The work of Terry Johnson is to be commended because it comes from one of the leading young pastors of America. It is pastoral, practical, and preeminently Reformed. The Independent Presbyterian Church of Savannah, Georgia, is one of the most beautiful historic churches in America, the crown jewel of Savannah's historic district. There one finds traditional Presbyterian worship with its emphasis on lectio continua expository preaching, psalmody, and family prayer. I know of no other church that so beautifully continues the tradition of Calvin, Knox, Baxter, and Matthew Henry.

What is refreshing is that the ministry of Terry Johnson has not only historical integrity but it has a very definite appeal to young people, proving once again that the genuinely classic is of interest to all, both the old and the young.

Hughes Oliphant Old

WHEN GRACE COMES ALIVE

LIVING THROUGH THE LORD'S PRAYER

by

Terry L. Johnson

Christian Focus Publications

Other books by the same author
published by Christian Focus Publications:

The Family Worship Book
When Grace Comes Home
When Grace Transforms

© Terry L Johnson
ISBN 1 85792 882 2

Printed in 2003
by
Christian Focus Publications Ltd,
Geanies House, Fearn,
Ross-shire, IV20 1TW,
Great Britain

www.christianfocus.com

Cover design by Alister MacInnes

Printed and bound by Mackay's of Chatham

Contents

To my mother and father,
whose hearth was the school of discipleship
in which I learned my first prayers.

I

Preliminaries

Foreword

What should we think of an army facing mighty foes in life and death battle that failed to employ its most effective weapons? How sympathetic would we be towards troops who were grieving their losses, and yet had neglected 'to crank up' their tanks, helicopters, missiles (or whatever)? Who would be surprised, or even compassionate, over such foolish defeat? It is doubtful that any military force in the world would ever be guilty of such horrendous negligence; but what about that 'mighty army, the Church of God'? I may be wrong, but it has long been my impression that much of the church has for too long failed to take up one of her mightiest weapons: 'all prayer' (listed in the spiritual weaponry of Eph. 6). In the United States, for instance, I lived through a time when the majority of evangelical churches closed their Wednesday night congregational prayer meetings (in the late 1950s and early 1960s). We laid down a mighty weapon just at the time our culture was exploding; just at the time when we had never more needed the timely blessings of the Spirit of God, who is given in answer to prayer (Luke 11: 13). I often wonder: would the Western nations have gone so secularist had the Church kept fervently praying?

But rather than lamenting past failures, it is best to confess sin (including prayerlessness), and by God's grace 'press forward unto those things which are ahead' (Phil. 3: 13). In a sense, the worst times are the best times, and from that perspective what tremendous opportunities open before us, if once again we press forward with 'the sword of the Spirit which is the Word of God' and the weapon of all prayer! We can scarcely imagine what local congregations and the whole Body of Christ (the Church militant!) will then be empowered to accomplish for the glory of Christ! And no doubt this is already happening in various parts of the world (especially, I think, outside 'the West').

I am delighted with Terry Johnson's *When Grace Comes Alive*, specifically because it could serve as a clarion call to humble and believing prayer in thousands of churches across the world. His book gives the clear and convincing rationale for taking up this neglected weapon of divine power, and assists us in doing so in a very realistic way. For he takes an honest, open-hearted and humble look at the difficulties of life in our secular culture, as well as our own weaknesses and struggles. He is our fellow pilgrim; fighting the same battles that we all do. Terry has been an effective pastor for many years in a large, historic church in the heart of a major port city, with challenges aplenty! Belief in Holy Scripture as the very Word of God written, and the practice of much prayer have been his mainstay, and God has not failed to bless significantly those exposed to his ministry.

Three things in particular remain with me from this fragrant exposition of the Lord's Prayer: first, the judicious, Biblical balance of this call to prayer. It is not a cheap way to get out of God what we want in order to please ourselves. On the contrary, it is the vital breathing of life lived in union with Christ, with an eye to the glory of God and the needs and welfare of others (and in that context, the needs of family and self will indeed be taken care of most graciously). Secondly, I sensed a gentle, and yet powerfully convicting summons to a deeper, more sincere, and universal endeavour to be like Christ in every relationship of life. That is the grounds for effective intercession (I John 3: 22 – 24). Every concern for true holiness has a way of throwing us back on the sheer grace of God, so that we look afresh to Jesus who is our holiness. When we feel at our most unworthy, and are driven afresh to Christ as our very righteousness and life, how many new springs of intercession come bubbling up! It is no surprise that things around us (and within us) strangely begin to change. Thirdly, I found his discussion of 'praying without ceasing' to be sensible and hopeful for us ordinary Christian folk. If this book blesses others as it has me, great good for the Kingdom of God will come from it!

Douglas F Kelly
September 2003

Acknowledgments

This book began as a series of sermons preached at the Independent Presbyterian Church in Savannah, Georgia, between July 1999 and July 2000 as part of a larger series of sermons on the Gospel of Matthew.

I am indebted to my secretaries, Debbie Parker, who translated my chicken scratch into standard English, giving the manuscript its original shape, and to Lesley Sadler, who labored to bring it into final form. Proofreading is a tedious and thankless job. Joan Paez endures both my spoken and written sermons every week at IPC and has done much to improve my grammar. Likewise my mother-in-law, Mrs Howard Hartley (Annette), has offered a number of helpful suggestions in her reading of this and other of my manuscripts.

I am grateful for the gracious people of the Independent Presbyterian Church, who have been charitable in receiving the content of this book as well as its predecessor on the Beatitudes, also a part of this series on Matthew, *When Grace Transforms*. Likewise they have served as the proving ground for my evolving understanding of prayer, kindly appreciating the prayers that arise from the convictions expressed in the following pages.

In addition, the leadership of IPC has understood my role as a minister of the gospel in such a way as allows significant time for study and writing on a weekly basis, as well as periodic study weeks throughout the year. Without that designated time, this and other writing projects could not have been completed.

A sizeable number of sources have been helpful in understanding Matthew 6:1-13 and Matthew 7:7-11. Among the commentators on Matthew, L. Morris, D. A. Carson, and R. T. France have been the most illuminating of the modern expositions; Calvin, Ryle, the incomparable Matthew Henry among those of previous generations. J. Stott and M. Lloyd-Jones are both, in their own ways, indispensable in their expositions of the Lord's Prayer found in respective works on the Sermon on the Mount. Among the books on the Lord's Prayer and prayer generally, Douglas Kelly's *If God Already Knows, Why Pray?*, Henry's *Method of Prayer*, Watt's *Guide to Prayer*, and J. I. Packer's exposition found in *I Want to be a Christian* have been the most valuable. I have tried to keep the text of this work uncluttered by indicating sources listed in the bibliography only with names and page numbers or simply page numbers.

The folks at Christian Focus have been a great encouragement to me. To my surprise and delight, they have appreciated my writing and encouraged it along. Throughout they have been patient with deadlines and my unending revisions. I owe much to William MacKenzie and his merciful staff.

My wife, Emily, and my five children have been wonderfully supportive throughout the writing and revising process. Our daily family devotions have also been an important context in which we have learned to pray as Jesus taught His disciples to pray.

Finally, the single most important factor in the shape and direction of my life is the fact that I was reared in a Christian home. My mother and father took me to Sunday School and church every Sunday from birth to adulthood. It was in their home that I realized personal faith in Christ and developed the central convictions that would define my life. To them this work is gratefully dedicated.

Introduction

'I know very little about prayer', I found myself thinking some time after my fortieth and before my forty-fifth birthday. Don't misunderstand. I had been taught to pray at home and in church as a child, cutting my spiritual teeth on the Lord's Prayer as well as that simple childhood prayer,

> God is great and God is good,
> Let us thank Him for our food...
> In Jesus name, amen.

I have often thought the whole mystery of providence is summed up in that opening line affirming both the greatness and goodness of God. Indeed, the whole problem of evil may be "solved" by denying either side of the equation (God is not great, so He can't prevent evil; God is not good, so He delights in evil). Instead our children are taught to affirm by faith this mystery from the very beginning.

In my early twenties I began praying fairly seriously, soon found myself leading others in prayer, and before too long was even teaching others to pray. Yet in my forties it began to dawn on me that I actually knew very little. My own outlook was evolving. I had begun my adult prayer pilgrimage with what I might call a 'prayer list' approach, repeating lists of objectives to

God in the hope of good results. On the other end of this pilgrimage I began to see that prayer is primarily *drawing near to God* (e.g. Jas. 4:8-10; Heb. 4:15, 16; 10:19-22). What am I doing in prayer? I am consciously moving into the presence of God. Prayer was evolving in my thinking from being primarily about requests (an experientially sterile idea) to being primarily about fellowship with God. Prayer is that time when I draw near to God to contemplate His greatness, search my soul, confess my sin, and plead for help. Prayer for me was becoming increasingly *personal, relational,* and *indispensable.* Moreover, it was also moving from being a discipline to be maintained with difficulty to being a privilege to be guarded jealousy.

There is no more vital subject for the disciple of Christ than prayer. There are other spiritual disciplines, and in Matthew's Gospel (our primary text for the Lord's Prayer) Jesus provides instruction paralleling that which He gives on prayer (6:2-4, 16-18). But on prayer alone He elaborates. Matthew Henry points out that this is because, 'In prayer we have more immediately to do with God' than in the other disciplines. Lloyd-Jones in his indispensable *Studies in the Sermon on the Mount,* says prayer is 'the highest activity of the human soul' before which all else 'pales into insignificance' (vol. 2; 45, 46). 'Man is at his greatest and highest when, upon his knees, he comes face to face with God', he insists (45). Robert Murray McCheyne's oft-quoted assertion rings true:

> What a man is alone on his knees before God, that
> he is – and no more.

The study of prayer is serious business. We can turn to no more valuable text than the Lord's Prayer, the most beloved and widely–used prayer ever composed. For generations the Lord's Prayer has taught the people of God how to pray. Serving as a *form* of prayer for the liturgy of the church, it has been recited countless times in the private and public services of the church, Protestant, Catholic and Orthodox. It has also served as a *pattern* for prayer, an outline of how we are to formulate our own prayers. It seems that Jesus had both uses in mind from the beginning. Presumably Jesus taught this prayer on numerous occasions and in various settings. In Luke's account of one of those occasions Jesus says, 'When you pray, say...' In other words, here are the very words you are to use. The disciples ask, 'Lord, teach us to pray', and He answers (in effect) 'Repeat these words after me', giving them the words of the Lord's Prayer as a *form* to be repeated (Luke 11:1-4). Matthew's setting is the Sermon on the Mount, and in this context Jesus says, 'Pray, then, in this way' or 'Pray like this'. The Lord's Prayer in Matthew is not a form but a 'perfect summary', a 'kind of skeleton' that 'covers everything' in outline form says Lloyd Jones (49). Apparently it can function in either way, as a prayer to be repeated verbatim, or as a 'model prayer to guide disciples in their devotional life', as Morris puts it (143). Indeed it has served the church well in both capacities.

The Lord's Prayer is both a simple prayer and yet comprehensive. All that we need to know is summarized in its few lines. Matthew Henry finds it to be 'remarkably concise and yet vastly comprehensive' (*A Method for Prayer*, 189). 'No part of Scripture is so full, and so simple at the same time as this', says J C Ryle (50). 'Never was prayer so admirably and curiously composed as this', notes Thomas Watson in his classic work *The Lord's Prayer* (1). 'He has mercifully supplied us with a simple yet comprehensive directory', notes Pink. 'Every part or aspect of prayer is included therein' (72). It is a 'breviary and compendium of the gospel', says Tertullian, 'a system or body of divinity', adds Watson (1). It is a gracious and kind thing that Jesus does in teaching us to pray. He condescends to our weakness and meets us in our need, providing in the words of Douglas Kelly, 'that most perfect form of prayer, "The Lord's Prayer"' (5).

I hope to impart something of what I am learning on the following pages. My aim is to provide an exegetically competent and thoroughly practical exposition of prayer as Jesus taught it and as we are meant to experience it.

1

Our Needs

As we begin our study of prayer, we should pay close attention to two crucial principles that are more assumed than stated. We would err significantly if we were to conclude that because these principles are implicit to our text rather than explicit we might safely ignore them. To the contrary, they set the context within which further instruction occurs. What are they? First we look at the introduction to Luke's version of the Lord's Prayer:

> And it came about that while He was praying in a certain place, after He had finished, one of His disciples said to Him, 'Lord, teach us to pray just as John also taught his disciples' (Luke 11:1).

Our Need of Instruction
The first implicit principle is that of our need of instruction. The disciples understood their need of instruction. This is why they asked, 'Lord, teach us to pray' (Luke 11:1). Jesus, for His part, was strongly directive in his teaching: 'And when you pray, you are not ... But you when you pray, go ... and when you are praying, do not use ... therefore, do not be like them ...

Pray then in this way' (Matt. 6:5-9). Clearly He thought that we need instruction. We need help. We need not make the mistake of thinking that we need no instruction on prayer, except for perhaps a few hints on technique. Prayer is sometimes seen as being so intensely personal as to be beyond the evaluation of others. 'Some Christians resent the analysis of prayer', notes Derek Thomas. Prayer is what we do when we pour out our hearts to God. How could such a thing be critiqued? How could it be done wrongly? How could it be improved? They act as though, Thomas continues, 'some sacred ground is violated when we begin to dissect prayer under a spiritual microscope' (7). Yet, the disciples asked 'Lord, teach us to pray'. They perceived their need of instruction. Jesus responded with teaching on the *place*, the *form,* and the *content* (or words) of prayer. Apparently we need to be taught all of these things.

Why? Why is it not enough for us merely to say *whatever* is on our hearts, *whenever* and *wherever* we feel like it? Because with respect to prayer and worship, when left to ourselves, we *never get it right*. We don't know how to pray. We don't know *what* to say or *how* to say it. Why? To answer that we have to go 'back to the garden' and reacquaint ourselves with the givens of human nature. Since Adam and Eve ate the forbidden fruit we've been off in the bushes with them, hiding from God. We are separated from God and alienated from Him (Col. 1:21). We are 'enemies' (Rom. 5:10). We are 'without God in the world' (Eph. 2:12).

Because this is so, *we have no natural inclination to pray*. God is light, but as Jesus said, by nature we are lovers of the darkness and haters of the light (John 3:19, 20). We have a natural aversion to God. We don't like Him. We don't want to have to deal with Him. We

don't seek Him (Rom. 3:10). We refuse to honor or
serve Him (Rom. 1:18ff). Even as redeemed people the
dregs of our old nature continue to weigh us down
with this antipathy. We have to haul our bodies out of
bed and drag them into our prayer closet because fallen
human nature, the remnants of which still plague us,
resists contact with God. It wants to flee from God,
not draw near to Him in prayer.

In addition *we are by nature error-prone with respect
to the things of God.* The human heart is inherently
idolatrous, a virtual factory of idols, as Calvin said.
Our reluctance to pray is really a reluctance to pray to
the true God, which even the redeemed have to
overcome. If fallen human nature has an opportunity
to fashion a false god, it will immediately pray to and
worship *that* god with great devotion. The Apostle Paul
teaches this in an extended passage in Romans 1:18-32.
There is no lack of religious expression in the world.
The problem, says Paul, is that we 'suppress the truth',
indulge in 'futile' speculations, and have 'exchanged
the glory of the incorruptible God for an image in the
form of corruptible man and of birds and four-footed
animals and crawling creatures'. We have 'exchanged
the truth of God for a lie, and worshiped and served
the creature rather than the Creator, who is blessed
forever' (Rom. 1:23, 25). The whole history of religion
is a history of idolatry: God conceived of falsely and
worshiped wrongly. It does not encourage us to think
highly of our ability to get things right.

If we think of God wrongly, we will pray wrongly
too. For example, if we conceive of God as an
impersonal, non-material essence, then we may pray
in a non-cognitive manner, with mental inactivity, with
trances and meditation, rather than actively. If we

conceive of God as ignorant or dumb, likely to misunderstand what we are requesting, then we may need to perform some sort of 'sympathetic' or 'imitative magic' in order to get Him to understand. We might have to act out our request. If we want fruitful harvests, then we may need to go up to the high places where we will be seen, and engage temple prostitutes so He'll get the idea that our interest is fertility. This is the way that humanity has reasoned. Or if we want Him to send down fire from heaven, maybe we will need to slash our arms and drip red, fire-like blood so He'll see us and imitate the same. That's what the prophets of Baal did on Mt. Carmel (1 Kings 18). Do we conceive of God as a wicked, capricious, or hateful god? If so we may need to offer up human sacrifices. At the heart of the issue is the kind of god to whom we pray. In what form does he want the requests made? Does he want words? Or does he want a child, as did Molech, the Canaanite fertility god? The point is, left to ourselves, left to follow our hearts, we will invariably get it wrong.

Third, and critical to the whole discussion, all this matters to God. It matters to Him what we think about Him. It matters to Him how we pray to Him. Again, one might have thought that the truly important thing is that we pray. Just so long as we are sincere, so long as we try, so long as we pray on occasion, that's all that matters. Given how busy and distracted we are, God should be pleased that we find time to pray at all. He's not. He's not pleased with any concept of Himself which we might have. He's not pleased with any prayers that we might offer. We might think that it ought not to matter to God, but it does. He is not pleased to receive any scraps of religious interest that we might offer to Him. He requires that we think of Him rightly, and that we approach Him rightly. Consequently, we must be taught. We need instruction. If we are wise we will realize with the Apostle Paul that 'we do not know how to pray as we should' (Rom. 8:26). With the disciples we will ask, 'Lord, teach us to pray.'

Our Need of Spiritual Discipline

The second implicit principle is our need of spiritual discipline. We may now move to Matthew's version of the Lord's Prayer, the fuller of the two, and the text upon which we will concentrate. Matthew 6 begins with an examination of the spiritual disciplines of giving, praying and fasting.[1] Prayer, we note, is among the disciplines that are not to be hypocritically practiced, but are to be practiced. Jesus says:

---

[1]There is a sense in which we can understand the entire fifth chapter of Matthew, the opening section of the Sermon on the Mount, as Jesus explaining what He meant by a 'righteousness' that 'exceeds' that of the scribes and Pharisees (5:20). The superior righteousness of the disciples of Christ is a *moral* righteousness. It is a righteousness of the heart as well as act. It is righteous character, as in the beatitudes (5:2-14), righteous conformity to the law of God, broadly not narrowly understood, internally as well as externally applied (5:16-48).

Jesus is still concerned with righteousness as we begin chapter 6. But though the word is the same, the meaning shifts. Whereas chapter 5 was concerned with righteousness as it applies to *ethics*, chapter 6 is concerned with righteousness as it applies to *religion*. Jesus says:

> Beware of practicing your righteousness before men to be noticed by them; otherwise you have no reward with your Father who is in heaven (Matt. 6:1).

What the NASV renders 'practicing your righteousness' (lit. 'doing your righteousness') the NIV translates 'doing acts of righteousness', the RSV, 'practicing your piety', the NEB, 'make a show of your

Beware of practicing your righteousness before men to be noticed by them; otherwise you have no reward with your Father who is in heaven (Matt. 6:1).

What do we learn from this?

First, Jesus assumes the importance of spiritual disciplines. He assumes the propriety and benefit of regular practices or disciplines such as giving, praying, and fasting. In Jesus' day the pious *gave* regularly and generously, tithing even the 'dill, mint and cumin' (Matt. 23:23); *prayed* three times a day as did Daniel before them (Dan. 6:10); and *fasted* twice each week (Luke 18:12), as well as during special holy seasons (e.g. the Day of Atonement, Lev. 16:29-31). These were what Barclay called the 'three cardinal works of the religious life, the three great pillars on which the good life was based' (I, 184). Prayers were offered at 9:00 am, 12:00 noon, and 3:00 pm. Weekly fast-days were Monday and Thursday. There was a routine, a discipline, an order to the practice of piety. The details of these routines were not normalized by Jesus for His disciples, except the general expectation that we are doing them at least in some degree. 'When therefore you...', Jesus says as he introduces giving, praying, and fasting (Matt. 6:2, 3, 5, 6, 16, 17). He assumes that His disciples will be

---

religion'. Stott says Jesus 'moves from a Christian's moral righteousness to his "religious" righteousness' (125). The subjects with which He is concerned in the verses that follow the introductory first verse are giving, praying, and fasting, 'the most prominent practical requirements for personal piety in mainstream Judaism', notes R. T. France (130). So a shift has occurred, from morality to religion, from ethics to the disciplines of piety. His words have 'special application to religious observance rather than to ethical obedience' says France again (131).

practicing these spiritual disciplines. While He does not attach numbers to them or endorse a schedule (give such and such an amount, pray and fast with such and such frequency), he offers no criticism of their disciplines as such. He will criticize their *ostentation* in giving, praying, and fasting, but not their *routine*. He chastises hypocrites who 'sound the trumpet' so as to be seen engaged in spiritual practices, but offers no criticism whatsoever for their discipline and order. The Lord's Prayer itself is a *daily* prayer ('give us *this* day our *daily* bread'). Jesus *assumes* that we too are regular in the practice of religious or spiritual exercises. Why would He expect this? It must be that there is spiritual benefit to be found in religious routines such as these. It should not surprise us then to find Peter and John continuing the pattern of piety in which they were reared, 'going up to the temple at the ninth hour, *the hour of prayer*' (Acts 3:1, my emphasis).

Spiritual growth, growth in piety (love for God, devotion to God), is fostered through regular use of spiritual disciplines. Piety grows as we regularly give, pray, fast, and meditate upon God's Word, participate in public worship, and so on. How is it that I will grow to be a strong Christian? How will I become a mighty man or woman of God, devoted to Christ, morally beyond reproach, and full of love and compassion for others? We need to be honest and clear about this.

It won't happen *automatically*. Spiritual maturity won't just drop out of heaven. God is unlikely to zap us with spiritual depth. It doesn't happen that way. He has given us *means* by which we are to grow in faith. Giving, praying, and fasting are three of them. There are others. But hoping for spiritual growth, or wishing for spiritual maturity is not going to produce the results. It won't happen through osmosis. It isn't automatic.

Neither is it likely to happen *spontaneously*. We live amidst a cultural bias favoring unplanned or spontaneous acts over those that are planned or routine. Somehow they seem to us more credible than those that arise from forethought and discipline. What previous generations might have seen as impulsiveness, we see as more authentic. The spontaneous toast (vs. the written one), the handwritten note (vs. the typed and corrected letter), the surprise dinner date (as opposed to a regularly scheduled one), all seem more sincere, more genuine, more 'real' to us. To say that an action was 'calculated' is to condemn it. Similarly, in relation to God, prayer or giving or fasting *when I feel like* praying or giving or fasting seems more authentic to us than a regular scheduled, planned discipline of such. Some make the mistake of neglecting spiritual disciplines for this very reason. They embrace, whether they know it or not, the assumption that a spontaneous, feeling-prompted relationship with God is superior to one ordered by the calendar and clock. That assumption, I am arguing, is false and undermines spiritual progress. Why? Because human nature, fallen in sin and hostile to God, cannot be depended upon to generate sufficient positive attitudes to foster spiritual growth. If I wait until I am internally motivated to pray, I may rarely, or perhaps I may never pray!

Since these two options are doomed to fail, let's move on to a third that will work.

Spiritual growth will take place as I faithfully use the God-given means of growth. J C Ryle forcefully asserts this principle in his tract, *A Call to Prayer.*

I believe that spiritual as well as natural greatness depends in a high degree on the faithful use of means within everybody's reach...when a man is once converted to God, his progress in holiness will be much in accordance with his own diligence in the use of God's appointed means. And I assert confidently that the principal means by which most believers have become great in the church of Christ is the habit of *diligent private prayer* (36, 37).

Prayer is to be a 'habit' that we pursue with diligence. When we don't feel like praying, pray anyway, and pray regularly. Does that open us up to the danger of formalism, of 'going through the motions', of embracing the form of prayer without its heart and soul? Yes, it does. That is why we ignore our feelings, and pray (or fast, etc.) not *mechanically* (as though God were a machine and not a person), and not *legalistically* (as though there were redemptive merit in praying), but honestly, acknowledging openly to God that our hearts are cold, distant, and far removed from Him, confessing the sin of it, and pleading for His Spirit to come and inflame our hearts. This is the kind of honesty we find in Isaac Watts' hymn, 'Come, Holy Spirit, Heavenly Dove'. He writes:

In vain we tune our formal songs,
In vain we strive to rise;
Hosannas languish on our tongues,
And our devotion dies.

And shall we then forever live
At this poor dying rate?
Our love, so faint, so cold to you,
And yours to us so great!

At this point, does he give up? Does this honest self-evaluation, which discovers spiritual formalism and coldness, result in passivity in the name of sincerity? No, he cries out for help!

> Come, Holy Spirit, heav'nly Dove,
> With all your quick'ning powers;
> Come, shed abroad a Savior's love,
> And that shall kindle ours.

Let's not make the mistake of failing to worship God in song or prayer merely because our hearts are cold. Instead acknowledge it and plead for help. 'Come, Holy Spirit!' we pray.

This applies to all the means of spiritual growth that God has given to His people. Do I make the mistake of going to church only when I feel like it? No, I make public worship, morning and evening, a part of my routine. It is automatic for me, like brushing my teeth. I don't always feel like doing it, but I do it anyway because I know that it is the right thing to do. When I arrive at church I find that my heart begins to warm as I pray before the service begins, as we are called to worship, as we sing the opening hymn, as the Scripture is read, and so on. As I obey the command by faith, my heart begins to follow.

The same may be said of Sabbath observance, daily family worship and daily personal devotions. We don't always feel like doing these things. But we make them a part of our routine. We place them permanently on our schedule knowing that they are means of grace, and praying that the Spirit will overcome our lethargy and bless us. Day in day out, Sabbath after Sabbath, we lay hold of Christ through the means of grace, and receive the blessing that He promises to those who seek

Him there. I believe that this is the true meaning of Paul's exhortation to 'pray without ceasing' (1 Thess. 5:17). Many a fervent sermon has been given on how we ought to pray twenty-four hours a day, by being in an attitude of prayer throughout the day, praying about everything that we encounter as it arises. That may or may not be good advice, but I doubt that this is the meaning of his command. The more natural and sensible understanding of his meaning is, 'don't stop your regular practice of prayer'. Continue your routine of daily intercessory prayer. Don't cease this important discipline. Continue to offer your prayers and don't compromise your regular routine. Don't let persecution, laziness, doubt, or unbelief get in the way of your daily (twice daily? three times?) prayers. Jesus is not urging us to pray in our sleep. He is urging faithfulness in our prayer commitments. 'Discipline yourself for the purpose of godliness', the Apostle Paul tells Timothy (1 Tim. 4:7).

The alternative of only praying when our hearts are right is not purer prayer and purer worship arising from purer hearts filled with purer motives, but no prayer. Utopian demands of ourselves will not result in a more wholesome practice of private prayer, family devotions, or public worship, but little or no prayer at all. Don't let the best get in the way of the achievable. I think it was Chesterton who said, 'Anything worth doing is worth doing badly'. If it is worth doing, it is worth doing even if it is done imperfectly. Pray for help.

A common complaint is that the requirement of daily prayer, or daily family devotions, or twice Sunday worship, can seem overwhelming, even oppressive. It can become a kind of tyranny, demanding things of us, filling us with guilt, robbing us of joy. Surely God doesn't want me in church on Sunday morning, sitting there hypocritically, when I'd rather be on the golf course! He doesn't want me to pray when I'd rather be sleeping! Feeling that I must do these things is oppressive and burdensome, we complain. But the fact that spirit disciplines may become burdensome is not inherent in the disciplines themselves, but in the manner of exercising them. Most of us have daily disciplines of personal hygiene and exercise. Brushing our teeth daily, even twice daily, is a regular part of our schedule and yet is not oppressive to us. As we've noted, Jesus offers no critique of spiritual routine and discipline *per se*. He does not direct us to a better alternative than regular spiritual disciplines. His criticism is entirely a matter of how they are being done – ostentatiously or mechanically. His solution is not to abolish corrupted disciplines but to urge that they be done correctly. 'When you pray do this and not that', etc. If they seem oppressive, our first response ought to be self-examination. Search our hearts. Why is a half-hour of television a breeze and fifteen minutes of family Bible-reading and prayer a burden? Hmmmmm? Why is a three-hour ball game like nothing and five minutes in prayer impossible? Why is regular exercise a pleasure (even though Scripture warns that it is 'only of little profit' [1 Tim. 4:8]) and regular devotions a tyranny? There are heart issues of great importance at stake here. The problem is not the disciplines (which are God-given and good), but us. Sometimes the spirit is willing and the flesh is weak, and so we fail in our prayers. Other times the spirit is not willing. That is the real problem. The real problem is that what ought to be a delight to us, is not. This points us to the larger principle which we shall take up in the next chapter.

2

Pleasing God in Prayer

And when you pray, you are not to be as the hypocrites; for they love to stand and pray in the synagogues and on the street corners, in order to be seen by men. Truly I say to you, they have their reward in full. But you, when you pray, go into your inner room, and when you have shut your door, pray to your Father who is in secret, and your Father who sees in secret will repay you (Matt. 6:5, 6).

Maintain the discipline of prayer, we have been saying so far. Don't throw the proverbial baby out with the bath water. Yet we must acknowledge that an undisciplined piety was not the issue with which Jesus was dealing. The religious leaders of His day and their disciples were disciplined enough. Their problem was that their religious discipline was hypocritical. They practiced their righteousness 'before men, to be noticed by them' (Matt. 6:1). That is the center of Jesus' critique and points to the larger principle that we have been anticipating. The disciplines of piety must be practiced for the right motive.

Typically *our* problem today is not discipline devoid of heart. The undisciplined modern church-goer seems far from the hypocrisy of the disciplined scribes and Pharisees of Jesus' day. Yet, ironically, they end up at the same place. Both have problems of the heart. To the former Jesus is saying, 'may God give you the desire (heart) to practice the disciplines of piety', to the latter He says, 'may you practice the disciplines of piety with the right motive'. To both Jesus is saying that acceptable prayer *aims at pleasing our Father in heaven.*

Just as Jesus was not criticizing spiritual disciplines *per se* but their abuse, neither was He attacking public prayers and offerings and services, as some have wrongly understood. Public services or ordinances of worship are endorsed, commanded, and modeled from Genesis to Revelation. Jesus is not abolishing congregational worship! What He is attacking is the corrupt motives that can accompany public acts of piety. The hypocrites that He critiques wished to be noticed by others. Their giving and praying and fasting were not sincere. They were publicly conducted in a way calculated to enhance their reputations. They were performing for a human audience.

Pleasing God

The key then for both private and public devotional disciplines is that they be exercised to please God. Your audience is 'your Father who is in heaven' who sees and rewards. Repeatedly Jesus speaks of 'your Father who sees in secret' (vv. 4, 6, 18). Do these things in secret, He says, so that you will not be corrupted by other motives. Have in view only His reward, and you will not be tempted to put on a religious act for whatever reward the world might offer. Whether a given discipline is practiced daily, weekly, or yearly, whether behind closed doors or on the public square, the crucial thing is that it is done to honor and serve

God. Lose that supreme motive, and you have lost all. Sneak into your prayer closet to honor *God*. Gather the family daily for prayers to serve *God*. Observe the Sabbath to please *God*. Assemble with the saints in public worship to glorify *God*. It is for *Him* that we give our tithes, offer our prayers, and fast. When this is our aim, then they are truly means of grace and result in spiritual progress.

Let us look now at the details of Jesus' criticism of 'street corner' prayer and commendation of 'secret' prayer. Remember as we do so that the larger goal is keeping pure our motives in prayer, that we pray only so as to please God.

First, do not pray for the sake of your own reputation. 'The Jewish system of prayer made ostentation very easy', notes Barclay. 'The Jews prayed standing, with hands stretched out, palms upward, and with head bowed' (196). It was easy for them to make spectacles of themselves. Hypocrites 'love' to go to a public place, 'in the synagogue and on the street corners'. To what end? For what purpose? It was 'in order to be seen by men'. They loved to put on a public religious act so that others would applaud their piety. Let's be sure that we understand what Jesus is saying and what He is not saying.

Jesus is not condemning *standing* for prayer. There are a variety of legitimate postures for prayer described in the Bible:

Standing (the usual posture) (1 Sam. 1:26; Mark 11:25; Luke 18:11, 13)
Kneeling (2 Chron. 6:13; Dan. 6:10; Luke 22:41; Acts 7:60, 9:40, 20:36, 21:5)
Sitting (2 Sam. 7:18)
Lying prostrate (Num. 16:22; Josh. 5:14; Dan. 8:17; Rev. 1:17, 4:10, 5:8, 5:14, 11:16)

Posture isn't irrelevant. Posture does count for something. There is a reverential pose which is appropriate to prayer and more generally for worship. Thus when the Psalmist calls us to worship he urges us to 'bow down' and 'kneel' (Ps. 95:6). I once heard John Stott say that slouching in prayer was an abomination to God. Presumably one would never assume that kind of flippant or casual posture in the actual presence of the Almighty. Neither should one in the prayer closet. But it is possible to reverentially and respectfully stand, kneel, sit, and lie prostrate. Our point is that it is not the standing *per se* to which Jesus objects.

Jesus is not condemning praying in *public*. As we noted above, public prayer is of divine institution. Prayer in the synagogue and even in the streets is legitimate. It could be that the pious were eager to bring religious expression into the public square in order to fight a secularizing trend. Remember pious Jews prayed three times a day at the hours of 9:00 a.m., 12:00 noon, and 3:00 p.m. They might unavoidably find themselves in a public space when the hours came. If so, there was nothing inherently wrong with praying in public, where one might be seen, whether in the synagogue or on the street corner. After all, Jesus begins in Matthew 6:9 to teach his disciples to pray '*Our* Father', which is not an individual, but group (i.e. public) prayer.

If standing in public to pray is not the problem, what is the problem? The problem is the temptations that accompany public prayer. Jesus is issuing a strong warning about our vulnerability to corruption. We are so likely to twist our motives for prayer when we pray publically that normally we ought to avoid it altogether. Here is how it sometimes happens: Perhaps you have been devout and earnest in your prayers all your life. But then one day someone makes a comment to you about your prayers. They say something like, 'I noticed how *often* you pray', or 'I am so impressed with how *long* you spend in prayer', or 'your prayers are so *beautiful*', or 'I so appreciate your *earnestness* in prayer'. Naturally, the human ego being what it is, you find that you like being complimented. Of course you were initially embarrassed by the comments. But it's nice to be appreciated. Very subtly a shift occurs. The next time you set out to pray, you do so wondering, even hoping, that someone is watching and will take note. You begin to gauge how long you'll pray based on what length will be impressive to others. You begin to calculate the wording of your prayers so as to generate a response. What has happened? You have begun to pray not to God but to the crowd. You are now praying 'so as to be seen'. Even in its subtle forms, this is deliberate ostentation in prayer, and is hypocritical.

Jesus calls them 'hypocrites' because they are pretending devotion to God when their true aim is 'to be seen by men'. They are deliberately placing themselves where they can be seen and heard. In Jesus' day they may even have been timing their movements so that when the hour of prayer came they would be in the most prominent of places. Thus they are pretending to be something they are not. A hypocrite pretends to be a devout man, a man of prayer. He plays the part. He stands there chattering his prayers. But it's all an act. He is insincere. His motives are self-serving and corrupt. He is praying *for himself,* not for God. Religion has become an exhibitionist display for him, supplanting the honor and glory of God as the end for which he worships.

Hypocrites, Jesus says, get their 'reward in full', right here and now. The applause of the crowd, the positive opinions of those who see them, the acclaim, the worldly recognition, is all that the hypocrites will ever get. They are like the man having an affair who brings flowers and candy home to his wife, and sends her notes, and buys her expensive things. He gives and does 'so as to be seen'. His actions are two-faced and hypocritical. He gets no credit for his presents. They are deemed worthless, even blameworthy, because they were not given in sincerity. His gifts, like the hypocrites' prayers, were self-serving and condemned. They appear to be expressions of love but are not.

Second, pray in secret.

> But you, when you pray, go into your inner room, and when you have shut your door, pray to your Father who is in secret, and your Father who sees in secret will repay you (Matt. 6:6).

Rather than praying in public where you might be tempted to pray 'so as to be seen', here is the alternative. 'But you', Jesus says, 'when you pray'. Of course you are going to pray. Of course you will have regular habits of prayer. Of course you will practice a consistent, regular routine of prayer. When you do, here is how to do it so as to avoid hypocrisy.

1. *Pray in secret.* Go to your 'inner room'. The houses of Palestine in Jesus' day typically had an interior room that was windowless, that served as a storeroom, and was the only safe room in the house. Go there and 'shut the door'. Why shut the door? Two

reasons: a) so that you can shut-out distractions and, b) so that you will remove the temptation to pray so as to be seen. Don't even let anyone know that you are going to your prayer closet. Don't let anyone know how often you go to pray or how long you stay. Human nature is so twisted and so perverse that you must remove every possible source of spiritual pride. Go to your closet, close the door, let no-one see you and let no one know. Now, do you lose motivation to pray? Are you easily motivated to pray at church, or in a small group, but not in the closet? If that is the case there is something wrong.

The same questions could be asked of a variety of religious activities. For example, why do you go to church? Or why do you attend Bible studies or prayer meetings? If it is to please and honor God, then why might the motivation to attend vanish when the crowd disappears? Why does the incentive dry up when your audience is absent? For some, the motivation to attend public religious ordinances is related to their interest in a crowd, or a group of two or three, or maybe even just one person. They develop a fascination with a particularly appealing person or group. They begin to appear at church every time the doors are open. They come to Sunday School, to morning and evening worship, to mid-week Bible study, and so on. Why? To see and be seen. This is hypocrisy. The answer is not to stop coming to public events, but to go to your closet, repent of self-serving idolatry, and pray in secret for a heart that hungers and thirsts for righteousness and is pure (Matt. 5:3ff).

2. *Pray to God.* This is the ultimate goal of secret, closed door, closet prayer. Shut out distractions and

eliminate any potential audience so that, without ulterior motives, you can *pray to God alone*. The point of prayer is to honor and please and know God.

For years my personal devotions were largely a routine. I had a 'quiet time' because I knew that I should. I had a prayer list and I knew that I should 'pray the list'. I feared *not* praying the list. Discipline alone sustained me for a number of years. But finally I found myself in an experiential desert. My soul was barren. Then one day I realized that in my closet prayers I was meant to actually 'connect'. That's the word that the Rev. Frank Barker of Briarwood Presbyterian Church once used. He had prayed a number of times in his life. But on one life-changing occasion, he 'connected'. Jesus says our Father 'is in secret'. Not only does He 'see in secret' but He is *there*, in the secret place of prayer, to be experienced and enjoyed.

Since the Father is there in the secret place, seek Him. This is what prayer is all about. 'Draw near to God and He will draw near to you' (Jas. 4:8-10). He says to us, 'Seek My face'. Get to where you can answer with integrity and passion, 'Thy face, O Lord, I shall seek' (Ps. 27:4, 8). Seek Him 'earnestly' (Ps. 63:1). Desire 'nothing on earth' besides Him. Seek Him with the conviction that His 'nearness' is your good (Ps. 73:25-26, 28). Go to prayer longing and yearning for the presence of God (Ps. 84:1, 2). Then seek His help through confessing your sin and offering your petitions (Phil. 4:6). Jesus says your Father 'is in secret' and 'sees in secret'. Like Jacob, seek Him and don't let go until He blesses you (Gen. 32:26).

3. *Pray looking only to God's blessing.* Jesus promises He will 'reward' us. What does this mean? Jesus doesn't elaborate, leaving us to speculate. Let me suggest the following:

i. *God Himself* is our reward. God's primary promise to us is not *something* but *Himself.* As we've just seen in the Psalms, the presence of God is the greatest reward we could have. To enjoy His fellowship is our greatest good. The godly in every era come to understand this. They say, 'O LORD, I love the habitation of Thy house, and the place where Thy glory dwells' (Ps. 26:8). They say, 'For with Thee is the fountain of life; in Thy light we see light' (Ps. 36:9). God Himself is our blessing.

> How blessed is the one whom Thou dost choose, and bring near to Thee, to dwell in Thy courts. We will be satisfied with the goodness of Thy house, Thy holy temple (Ps. 65:4).

To be brought 'near' to God is to be 'blessed', the Psalmist says. His goodness brings satisfaction. 'O satisfy in the morning with Thy lovingkindness', he says (Ps. 90:14). The Bible is full of rich, experimental language in describing our relationship with God. In His presence we find the 'fullness of joy'. At His right hand are 'pleasures forevermore' (Ps. 16:11). I recently had a conversation with a man who said that twenty years after his conversion he had 'no personal relationship with Christ'. He said that his prayer life was completely perfunctory. He had no 'feelings'. His devotional life, in so far as it still existed, was devoid of any experiential dimension at all. This is not only a sad condition to be in, but also one for which we cannot settle. After wrestling with God, Jacob eventually says,

'I have seen God face to face' (Gen. 32:30). This must be our goal. My counsel was: seek the Lord until you find Him.

> Seek the Lord while He may be found; call upon Him while He is near (Isa. 55:6).

God will not withhold Himself from those who seek Him. Seek the blessing of His presence in everything from your closet prayers to public prayer. Don't stop seeking Him until you experience it. Don't settle for a formal routine – privately or publicly. Plead with God that you want fellowship with Him, that you want Living Water and the Bread of Life to satisfy your soul. Jesus intentionally uses this language of satisfaction and fulfillment to describe how we experience Him. 'If any man thirsts', Jesus says, 'let him come to me and drink' (John 7:37; cf. John 4:7-15; 6:35). He is able to quench the hunger and thirst of the soul. You can enjoy fellowship with the Triune God, Father, Son, and Holy Spirit (1 John 1:3).

ii. *Answered prayer is our reward.* The ostentatious prayers of Pharisees will never be answered. Our corrupt, self-serving prayers will never prevail. But when we purge our souls of ego-driven piety, and offer prayers that are not perfect but are genuinely sincere, God hears and God answers. Jesus said:

> And whatever you ask in My name, that will I do, that the Father may be glorified in the Son. If you ask Me anything in My name, I will do it (John 14:13, 14).

Ask anything 'in My name', that is, for Christ's glory and through Christ's power (as opposed to asking for personal glory and personal ends), and He will grant our requests. Similarly James says:

> You do not have because you do not ask. You ask and do not receive, because you ask with wrong motives, so that you may spend it on your pleasures (Jas. 4:2b-3).

Prayer works. Sometimes we 'do not have' because we 'do not ask'. When we ask, we have. Prayer really does change things. But there is the problem of corruption again. James says we ask with 'wrong motives'. Yet the implication is that when we ask with right motives, the real point of secret prayer, God hears and God answers.

Faith in prayer, or more accurately, faith in the God who answers prayer, is a real battleground for us today. It is crucial that we all understand the times in which we live. Our day is dominated by a secular and materialistic outlook. Reality for modern people consists of only those things which we can see, handle, taste, and touch. The 'bottom line' truly is the bottom line. We have extraordinary trouble believing in the unseen world, the world of God and demons, of heaven and hell. So we tend to live for now and for things. Eternity is largely forgotten. We approach what some have called 'practical atheism'. Consequently, devoting time to prayer is exceptionally difficult for us *because we struggle to believe that it really makes any difference*. But Jesus says that our Father is in secret and He sees us. Jesus says He hears our prayers. Though there is no one else to congratulate us, He will give us a 'reward'.

iii. *A changed heart is our reward*. Douglas Kelly devotes a whole section of *If God Already Knows, Why Pray?* to the theme 'Prayer Changes Us'. The primary thing in prayer is not getting answers to our petitions. Prayer is not us twisting the arm of God, compelling Him to do that which He would not otherwise do. In all our prayers we pray according to His will (1 John 5:14, 15). We always pray, 'Thy will be done'. This means that often prayer is a time when, through communion with God, we come to know ourselves better, Him better, have more light, and are more accepting of, and conformed to, His will. In the presence of the Holy One we are purged and purified. His word judges the 'thoughts and intentions of the heart' (Heb. 4:12). 'Search me, O God, and know my heart', we pray. 'Try me and know my anxious thoughts; and see if there be any hurtful way in me' (Ps. 139:23, 24). As we enjoy communion with God, His virtue rubs off on us, just as it does with our fellow human beings. When I was at Trinity College in Bristol, England, I so wanted just to hang around with my Principal, Hebrew teacher, and Old Testament lecturer, Alec Motyer, that I endured a summer of intense Hebrew just so that I could take more classes from him. I wanted to learn from him and be more like him. The only way to do that was to be with him. So it is with God. As we meet with God in prayer (and public worship as well!) His virtue 'rubs off'. We become more like Him. Our hearts are changed.

Third, do not pray mindlessly.
Jesus has already told the disciples not to pray ostentatiously, like the hypocrites do (Matt. 6:5). Here He adds another caution, this time drawn from paganism.

1. Do not use 'meaningless repetition'.

And when you are praying, do not use meaningless
repetition, as the Gentiles do, for they suppose that
they will be heard for their many words (Matt. 6:7).

The KJV translated this 'vain repetitions'. The
underlying Greek word, *battalogeō*, is very rare. It
may be onomatopoetic, like our word 'babble', the
Scots word 'blether', and the Greek word 'barbarian'.
The ba-ba-ba is what one hears listening to foreigners.
It sounds meaningless or senseless. Don't use
meaningless, senseless repetition. This is what the
'Gentiles' or pagans do. They 'heap up empty phrases'
(RSV). They repeat magic words, chants, mantras, over
and over again, mindlessly repeating sounds.

2. Do not use endless repetition.

Matthew uses a second
word at the end of verse 7, *polulogia,* 'many words'.
They may be synonymous. But if they are nuanced,
the first emphasizes the use of *meaningless* words, the
second the use of *many* words. In this case the pagans
think that God hears and grants their requests for their
'many words'. They pray on and on and on, as though
God could be coerced by the sheer volume of words.

It is not that long prayers are forbidden. Jesus spent
a 'whole night' praying (Luke 6:12). Neither is
repetition being forbidden. Jesus repeated himself three
times in the Garden of Gethsemane (Matt. 26:44).
Daniel passionately cries out to God to hear and listen
and see as he pleads for national forgiveness and
restoration (Dan. 9:18). Psalm 136 repeats 'His mercy
lasts forever' in every other line. The seraphim in
heaven cry out, 'Holy, Holy, Holy' (Isa. 6:1ff). But

Biblical repetition is limited to a few words or a few lines (it does not go on for minutes or hours) and is found in only these few places. Biblical prayer and praise make sparing use of repetition. This is worth considering when evaluating the gospel song and Scripture chorus genre. *Extensive* repetition is not only not encouraged, but discouraged in Christian worship by Jesus's words here. Yet, when moderately employed, it is permitted and Jesus is not prohibiting it.

What then is being forbidden? Extensive and mindless repetition, and the misconception of God to which both errors point. Pagans are attempting to do one or all of the following with their *batalogia* and *polulogia*:

- *inform God* – they view God as unaware, unconcerned, lofty and removed, or perhaps just ignorant (though powerful!). Consequently, they must repeat requests over and over to be sure that He gets it right;
- *persuade God* – God, they think, is reluctant to hear the prayers of His people or grant their requests. He is not a good god or a kind and loving god. No, he must be battered by a huge volume of words into doing what we want;
- *obligate God* – prayer is viewed as a meritorious work which, when performed sufficiently, obligates God to answer. God is reduced to a calculating judge or a machine, for whom prayer quotients are fulfilled in exchange for the desired gifts;
- *manipulate God* – words are viewed as having magical power. Certain verbal formulas unlock the power of the deity, who is an impersonal force.

In other words, repeat the right words in the right amounts and the god responds. This is how pagans pray. On and on and on they chant or repeat their formulae, seeking to inform, or persuade, or obligate, or manipulate their gods. The prophets of Baal for half a day cried out, 'O Baal, answer us' (1 Kings 18:26). For two hours the devotees of Artemis in Ephesus cry out, 'Great is Artemis of the Ephesians' (Acts 19:34). Barclay notes that Muslims are known to 'go on repeating the sacred syllable HE for hours on end, running round in circles, until they drive themselves to ecstasy, and finally fall down unconscious in total exhaustion' (196). For many of us the scenes of militant Muslims in the Middle East shouting 'Allah is Great' for hours on end is as fresh as the daily news.

Stott's question is the relevant one – what sort of gods are these? They are not the infinite, personal Father who knows or cares. Rather, they are forces which can be manipulated by words and magical incantations. They are powers which can be coaxed, or pestered, or battered through repetition into doing our will.

This is not just a pagan problem. Christians can make the same mistake, and they can make it both in churches that practice liturgical worship as well as those which practice what is called 'free' worship. Neither written nor extemporaneous prayers are exempt from falling into the same trap of thinking that either the form of words or 'mere length will make prayers efficacious' (Carson, 166); of thinking, as Morris puts it, that God answers prayer 'in proportion to (our) wordiness' (142). If we are thinking that God hears and answers in response to the time spent in prayer, or the length of our prayers, or the number of words used, or the precise phrasing, then we have misunderstood both prayer and God! Sometimes we view prayer like pagans. We frantically repeat requests lest God forget. We seek to persuade because we view Him as cruel or uncaring. Sometimes the view is that of merit – God will grant the request because I will have merited an answer through my lengthy prayers. In other words, when I jump through the prayer hoops, God's power must act on my behalf. You have no doubt heard it said, and perhaps said it yourself about a given matter – 'But I prayed so much about it'. In other words, 'How could things not have gone my way when I put so much prayer time into it?' Wasn't God obligated to honor such efforts? such sincerity? such earnestness? The answer, of course, is no. You are not heard for your 'many words'. God cannot be obligated by words, whether by magical formulae or by meritorious prayer-works.

Fourth, pray to Our Father who knows all things.
The problem with the pagan approach to prayer is addressed directly by Jesus: don't do it!

> Therefore do not be like them; for your Father knows what you need, before you ask Him (Matt. 6:8).

'Do not be like them', He says. Why not? Because our God is not that kind of God. He is a person, not a machine, or a power, or a force. He is a Father. 'Your Father knows', that is, He is aware, and by implication, He cares. He has noticed and is aware. He is concerned about it. He 'knows what you need before you ask Him'. Then how are we to pray?

1. Pray with a dependent heart. When we pray we are demonstrating our dependence upon God our Father in heaven. Prayer, as we shall see, is not a matter of approaching God with our shopping lists. We draw near to God in prayer to acknowledge through worship and praise that He is the great God who has made us, who sustains us, and supplies all our needs. He is the God 'in whom we live and move and exist' (Acts 17:28). He gives 'every good and perfect gift' (Jas. 1:17). He 'gives to all life and breath and all things' (Acts 17:25). Consequently, we go to Him in prayer in order to honor and worship Him, and to seek from Him that which He alone can provide. The act of praying implies our conviction that we are dependent upon God for those things which we seek.

2. Pray with an open heart. When we pray we are casting all our burdens upon our Father. The act of praying implies our faith that He is able and willing to hear and grant our requests. So we go to him with our needs: we are burdened with guilt for our moral and spiritual failures; we are weary from conflict with the devil, the flesh, and the world; we are anxious about the souls of our children; we are concerned about our ability to provide daily bread; we fear the future and the unknown; we long to lead holy and loving lives, lives conformed to the Beatitudes (Matt. 5:3ff), lives characterized by the fruit of the Spirit (Gal. 5:17ff). We take all our fears, all our concerns, all our needs, all our anxious longings, all our desires, all our hopes and aspirations, and we place them all in the lap of our Almighty Father. We are not informing One who is likely to forget; we are not persuading One who is callously reluctant; we are not obligating an uncaring scorekeeper; we are not manipulating an unthinking force. We are pouring out our hearts to our Father. He, in turn, promises to answer when we pray in this fashion, like a child to a Father. Thus we come to Him by faith, believing that He is able to resolve those matters that are upon our hearts.

3. *Pray with a believing heart.* When we pray we are using the God-ordained and approved means of grace. There is a connection between our requests and His gifts. This is why Jesus says:

> 'Ask, and it shall be given to you; seek, and you shall find; knock, and it shall be opened to you. For everyone who asks receives, and he who seeks finds, and to him who knocks it shall be opened' (Matt. 7:7, 8).

We pray with confidence that there is a certain relation between asking and receiving, seeking and finding, knocking and opening. As we've seen, it is so certain that James says, 'you have not because you ask not' (Jas. 4:2). Our Father hears our prayers and grants our requests. Prayer is a means by which we receive the gifts that our Father has to give us.

How long should we pray? The length of our prayers is only a reflection of the amount of time that it takes to pick up our burdens off our shoulders and place them on His. Rarely does this happen easily. Quick, formulaic prayers usually leave our burdens on us. We lack the faith that is necessary to take them to Him and leave them there. No, normally the process takes time, with cries, and groans, and pleadings. This is so, not because He won't hear and won't answer, but because *we won't let go*. And when we won't let go, it is because we lack faith. Isn't this obvious? We don't trust Him to hear and handle it. We struggle to believe that it is true. Does He really hear? Does He really care? We are filled with doubt. So we cling to our fears and pray without faith. Perhaps we have an unbelieving and rebellious child. So we come to our Father and we pray, 'O Lord, my son is in rebellion, his heart is hardened, he is in bondage to sin and I am so afraid. I fear he will destroy himself. I fear he will end up amongst the damned in hell.' So I cry out, 'O Lord save him.' But I have doubts. So I pray on. 'You are able to open blind eyes. You are able to raise the dead. Remember your promise to be a God to me and to my children. Don't let this child be lost. Deliver him! Save him! Rescue Him by Your power and grace.'

What have you done? You have spoken to your Father from your heart. You have struggled to give your concern to Him. And finally, you have given Him your burden. You have pled with Him and told Him all about it, not because He doesn't know or is reluctant, but because only through prayer are you able to give it over to Him, the One who is able to save your child. As you have done so, your faith has been strengthened, you have let it go, and have been comforted. He, for His part, hears and will answer! Let me provide an example.

The Rev Charles Amicy, Haitian Presbyterian pastor, provides a noteworthy example of persistence in prayer. Reared in a poor, farming family in northern Haiti, Charles from his youth had an insatiable hunger for education. Begging his mother for the opportunity to complete high school (most Haitian children are educated only through the sixth grade), and bribing

God (promising God that he would be a pastor if he would provide for his schooling), Charles finally did graduate – and promptly headed for the legal profession. The Lord, who has His ways, spun him around and at the age of twenty-nine sent him to Greenville Presbyterian Theological Seminary in the fall of 1995. Knowing no one, no English, and having no resources, the predictable happened. Charles was lost in his seminary courses, unable to communicate with anyone in his own language, and after three months plunged into despair, determined to return to Haiti. But before he left he decided to devote a morning to prayer. The designated day arrived and he cried out to God from 6 a.m. until noon. How long should one pray? Long enough to unload one's burden. This was no mere 'guide our steps' prayer. All morning long he poured out his heart to God searching and pleading for two things – someone to speak to in his own language and some way of learning English. He finally rose from his knees to discover that a phone call had come for him while he was praying. When the call was returned that evening, on the other end was a voice speaking French. The following day, the head of the language department at Bob Jones University called, also speaking in Charles' native tongue. Through this contact Charles began to learn English and to understand his seminary classes, earning outstanding grades while at the same time working twenty-five hours a week to support his family in Haiti. In the summer of 1998 he returned to Haiti. Five years later there are now five of the very first Haitian Presbyterian churches to be planted in that country, three Christian schools, a Bible School and a pharmacy. The churches minister to 1,000 attendees and the schools to 500 students. From passion and persistent prayer all this has come.

We pray to our Father. We pray in the confidence that He is our Father. We pray to please Him. We pray with as much length and intensity as is necessary to rise from our knees convinced that He knows, hears, and cares. Calvin summarizes the point like this:

'But if God knows what we need before we seek it, there might appear to be no benefit in prayer. If of His own accord He is ready to help us, what need have we to interject our prayers that might get in the way of the spontaneous course of His providence? There is an easy answer in the very purpose of prayer. The faithful do not pray to tell God what He does not know, or urge Him to His duties, or hurry Him on when He delays. Rather they pray to alert themselves to seek Him, to exercise their faith by meditating upon His promises, unburdening their cares by lifting themselves into His bosom. Finally they pray to testify that from Him alone, all good for themselves and for others is hoped for and asked. As for Himself, what He has determined to give of His own free will, and even before He is asked, He promises to give all the same, in response to our prayers. Keep hold of both points, then: our prayers are anticipated by Him in His freedom, yet, what we ask we gain by prayer' (vol. 1, 204).

II

The Preface of Praise

3

Our Father

The Lord's Prayer may be divided into 3 sections:

Preface – Matthew 6:9
Petitions – Matthew 6:10-13a
Benediction – Matthew 6:13b

The *preface* orients us to the One whom we are addressing: *'Our Father in heaven'*.

The *petitions* may be divided into two sections:

God's concerns – 6:9-10 – Hallowed be Thy name, Thy kingdom come, Thy will be done, on earth as it is in heaven;
Our concerns – 6:11-13 – Give us this day our daily bread. And forgive us our debts, as we also have forgiven our debtors. And do not lead us into temptation, but deliver us from evil.

The *benediction* is a rich ascription of praise: 'For Thine is the kingdom, and the power, and the glory, forever, Amen'. So the 'Lord's Prayer', the prayer which Jesus our Lord taught, begins with praise and ends with praise, a fact which in itself is instructive, and about which we shall have more to say later. Matthew Henry summarizes the Lord's Prayer in this way:

> The Lord's Prayer (as indeed every prayer) is a letter sent from earth to heaven. Here is the inscription of the letter, the person to whom it is directed, *our Father;* the place where, *in heaven;* the contents of it in several errands of request; the close, *for thine is the kingdom;* the seal, *Amen;* and if you will, the date too, *this day.*

Our immediate focus is the preface to the prayer:

'Our Father, who art in heaven'.

The preface to the Lord's Prayer is meant to orient us to the whole manner in which God is to be approached in prayer. The preface identifies our *perspective* in prayer; who we are in relation to the One to whom we are praying. It sets the tone, the mood for the whole prayer, and more broadly, for the whole of the Christian life. It is very accurate to say, as we pray so we live. Or again, as we relate to God in prayer, so also we relate to Him in all of life. As God is identified and addressed by Jesus, we understand how we are to approach Him and relate to Him. We may identify two fundamental principles: *intimacy,* God is my *Father;* and *transcendence,* God is my *heavenly* Father, whose name is to be hallowed. The first is our concern in this chapter.

A Covenantal Prayer

It is noteworthy that Jesus prays not 'my' Father, the singular, but the plural. 'Our' points to the communal or covenantal dimension of our relationship with God.

This is not to deny the individual privilege of calling God 'my' Father. Certainly God is personally my Father in Christ and I am His adopted son (Gal. 4:7). But the emphasis here is upon the communal. God has saved us not in isolation, not to leave us alone, but in the context of the body of Christ, into which we are incorporated and in which our prayers are offered. This prayer 'is meant to be prayed in community', notes Morris (144). When we pray, we pray with and for fellow believers.

The Lord's Prayer, then, assumes that we have received the gift of adoption. God is not my Father by birth, except in the broad sense as Creator (Mal. 2:10, Acts 17:28). God does not become my Father in the familial sense, as that one who loves and cares for me, except in Christ. 'But as many as received Him', writes the Apostle John, 'to them He gave the right to be children of God, even to those who believe in His name' (John 1:12). Further, he says, 'who were born not of blood, nor of the will of the flesh, nor of the will of man, but of God'. This is a *family* prayer, given by Jesus the natural Son to all the adopted sons and daughters who have been born again into the household of God (Eph. 2:19).

Further, Jesus assumes that His disciples are related by covenant to other believers. In other words, by praying '*Our* Father', He assumes the whole covenantal structure of the Bible, where God makes promises to His people, *and they in turn make promises to Him and to each other.* He assumes that they are bound to Him by covenant *and to each other* so that they can say of God, not only that He is *my* God, but that He is *our* God. He is *my* God, in that I am in covenant with Him, and He is *our* God in that *we have together made promises to Him and to each other.*

A fundamental element of the Christian life, including our prayer life, is our relation to *each other* in the church. We call upon God as *our* Father, not merely because we all happen to be sitting in the same room at the same time as a prayer begins. We do so because in the church we are bound by covenant to *each other*. The church, for its part, is not merely an invisible entity (though the invisible and universal dimension of the church's identity is of vital importance), but an actual *place* (e.g. 'to the church *at* Corinth') with actual *people*, to whom I have made real *promises*. To be a Christian is to be a member of the body of Christ. We belong to one another. We are committed to one another. We are saved out of the world and called into the church, the **ekklēsia**, the 'called-out ones'. There we cry out with others, 'Our Father'. There we are united with other believers, now as brothers and sisters looking dependently to a common Father. Together, those who were once strangers are now mutual members of the family of God, and now pray with each other and for each other saying, 'Our Father'. There we submit to the rule of God-given and godly elders, enjoy the administration of the means of grace, join in a family meal, under a common government with the keys of the kingdom and the power of binding and loosing (Matt. 16:19). There we love one another (John 13:35), bear one another's burdens (Gal. 6:2), serve one another (Gal. 5:13), encourage one another (Heb. 3:13), and pray for one another saying 'Our Father' (Jas. 5:16).

A classmate of mine in seminary said tongue-in-cheek to another student, 'you need to get an ecclesiology'. He perceived a weak view of the institutional church in his classmate. In this one word, 'our', we find in seed the whole doctrine of the church, including the theology of church membership and vows of membership. If when we kneel to pray we begin '*Our* Father', then our covenantal relationship to each other is of critical importance. If we cannot privatize this, the most personal of religious activities, our prayers, then what shall we say of the rest? '*Our* Father' identifies us as members of a family, with interests in one another. This is one of our highest privileges and greatest responsibilities.

A Family Prayer

Our mutual God is to be addressed, by the adopted members of the family, as '*Father*', says Jesus. That is, we have entered into a paternal, familial relationship with the Almighty Creator of heaven and earth. It means that He is a personal Father, intimate with His people in general and with each of us in particular. This is something new and wonderful. In addressing God in this manner, Jesus is revealing 'a new understanding of the nature of God', says Morris (144). It is not that God had never been thought of as a Father. The fifth and sixth of the Jewish prayers (known as the *Eighteen Benedictions)* address God as Father. Among the Greeks, Zeus was sometimes called 'Father Zeus'. But as Carson points out, 'not until Jesus is it characteristic to address God as Father' (169). Even in the Old Testament, where God is identified several times as Father (e.g. Deut. 32:6; Ps. 103:13; Isa. 63:16; Mal. 2:10), it is 'commonly by way of analogy, not direct address', argues Carson (169). It is Jesus who taught us to think of and pray to God as Father.

What does this mean for us? It means that we can pray with confidence of God's care. Note that Jesus does not teach us to pray 'O Great Ground of Our Being'. God is not some impersonal Force or imperturbable Power. Neither does He teach us to pray to lesser, and presumably more accessible, entities such as saints or angels. No, God is as accessible to us as is any good Father. Nor does Jesus teach us to pray to 'Our Mother'. The Fatherhood of God is no mere convention or an expendable, culturally relative metaphor. Human fatherhood was not merely a convenient analogy which Jesus employed, but which actually tells us nothing at all about what God is in Himself. The Biblical writers argue in the opposite direction, saying, not that God's Fatherhood is like ours, but that ours is like His. His is the original and the archetype upon which ours is modeled. The Apostle Paul writes:

> For this reason, I bow my knees before the Father, from whom every family in heaven and on earth derives its name (Eph. 3:14, 15).

He is the Father upon whom all subsequent Fatherhood is based. He provides the pattern for our own. Consequently, this designation, 'Father', is not relative or expendable or alterable. To state the obvious, what Jesus says becomes the norm for us. When we call upon God, we call upon Him as Father, not Mother or anything else. 'The knowledge of God's Father-love is the first and simplest, but also the last and highest lesson in the school of prayer', says Andrew Murray in his classic *With Christ in the School of Prayer* (31).

Let us then elaborate what is implied in addressing God as Father.

1. *We pray conscious of the grace of adoption.* We come to God as those who in Christ have received His grace, have been rescued from the damnation that we deserved, and are touched with a profound spirit of thanksgiving and gratitude. We pray with a spirit of wonder and amazement that He has saved us, and not only saved us but adopted us into His own family. Listen to the Apostle Paul recall in wonder that, 'He loved *me*, and delivered Himself up for *me*' (Gal. 2:20). Listen to the Apostle John explain, 'Behold what manner of love the Father has given unto us, that we should be called children of God' (1 John 3:1). That is it. We pray with the wonder that 'we should be called children of God', that we should be adopted into the family of God and now have the 'spirit of adoption as sons by which we cry out, "Abba, Father"' (Rom. 8:15, 16; Gal. 4:6). Beyond that He gives us His Spirit to help us in our weakness 'for we do not know how to pray as we should, but the Spirit intercedes for us with groanings too deep for words' (Rom. 8:26). Furthermore, Jesus promises that whatever we ask in His name 'that will I do' (John 14:13, 14). Can you imagine? Do you realize what an extraordinary privilege this is?

It would be enough if Christ were only to save us from hell and let us be heaven's street sweepers. But instead He accepts us and takes us into the family. He permits us to call Him Father. He invites us to pray to Him by that name. If we don't know how to pray, He not only provides this instruction, but also sends His Holy Spirit (the third person of the Holy Trinity, no less) to assist us, and even to intercede for us. Then He promises not only to hear, but to grant our requests. We have grown too accustomed to these truths. We have not pondered these privileges sufficiently. How can it be that I have been so elevated, so blessed? God is my Father! I am His son! He has granted to me the privilege of calling upon Him as Father! Amazing! And if we have not *pondered* these things sufficiently, we've not *practiced* them adequately either. Have we exercised our privilege? Do we turn to Him in prayer? Do we draw near to our Father? Do we realize this great gift that is ours and use it? Do we call upon God, 'Our Father', as His son? We pray not presumptuously, as though we, of course, have the right to call upon God as our Father. Rather we pray with gratitude and in awe that such a privilege should have been extended even to us.

2. *We pray confident of our Father's pity.* The Psalmist writes:

Just as a father has compassion on his children, so the Lord has compassion on those who fear Him (Ps. 103:13).

Because God is our Father, we pray with confidence that He looks upon us and our requests with sympathy. He knows our limitations. He understands the weakness of our prayers. The next verse in Psalm 103 says:

For He Himself knows our frame; He is mindful that we are but dust (Ps. 103:14).

He knows we are not made of steel or marble, as Thomas Watson points out. He is 'mindful' that we are 'but dust'. We come to Him with our flawed lives and flawed petitions. We are permeated by weakness and corruption. We pray not as we ought, and live not as we ought. We stumble. We fall. We fail. How does God look at us? As a Father does His children. He looks upon us with compassion. What could be more liberating than this? What could be more freeing and healing than to know that God is my Father? What could be more therapeutic than to know that He looks upon me, with all my 'brokenness and strife' with sympathy, with pity, with compassion? He is mindful that we are but dust. He takes it into account. He considers it. 'Like as a Father pitieth His children, so the Lord pitieth them that fear Him' (KJV). He is not like the mine foremen (or Egyptian taskmasters) that brook no excuses, ignore extenuating circumstances, accept no explanations, but ever demand more and more out of us. No. He understands. Is this not the way of good human fathers? We distinguish between what we expect of our 2-year-olds, our 10-year-olds, and our 20-year-olds. We take into account age, maturity, and physical limitations. We are mindful of differing capacities and abilities. We don't demand that our 2-year-olds assume the responsibilities of 10-year-olds. We view these limitations with understanding and sympathy. So it is with our Father in heaven. He knows. He sympathizes, as a Father does with His children. In our afflictions He is afflicted (Isa. 63:9).

This gives us great liberty in prayer, does it not? I am welcome, as a good Father welcomes His children. He hears, as a good Father listens to His children. This is not to deny that there are times when God is displeased with us, and I am the object of His righteous anger (Ps. 60, 77, 88, 90). Is it not so with good fathers? Do wayward children not grieve their fathers (Eph. 4:30)? Do good fathers not chasten their disobedient children (Heb. 12:5ff)? Of course, and we'll look at this more closely later. In the meantime, we remember that 'His anger is but for a moment, His favor is for a lifetime' (Ps. 30:5). Can you see how adoption is the key to understanding the Christian life? Can you understand also that while God is displeased with his rebellious children His unchanging disposition is that of a loving and sympathizing Father? So then I bring this outlook with me to my prayer closet. As I confess my sins, as I admit my wrongdoings, as I grieve over my errors, as I set my needs before Him, as I express my wants and desires, I do so to a loving and sympathizing Father. He in turn does not mock me, or begrudge my requests, but ever looks upon me with compassion.

3. *We pray confident of the Father's protection.* The Proverbs say:

> In the fear of the Lord there is strong confidence, and his children will have refuge (Prov. 14:26).

He is our refuge and our stronghold. Because God is my Father, I pray knowing that I am assured of His protection. The Psalmist writes:

> God is our refuge and strength, a very present help in trouble. Therefore we will not fear, though the earth should change, and though the mountains slip into the heart of the sea; though its waters roar and foam, though the mountains quake at its swelling pride (Ps. 46:1-3).

Again, he writes:

The Lord is my rock and my fortress and my
deliverer, my God, my rock, in whom I take refuge;
my shield and the horn of my salvation, my
stronghold. I call upon the Lord, who is worthy to
be praised, and I am saved from my enemies (Ps.
18:2-3).

We are 'kept by the power of God' (1 Pet. 1:5). He is
able to keep us from falling (Jude 24). He promises
never to leave or forsake us (Heb. 13:5). This is the
argument of Romans 8. The Spirit that He has given
to us is the Spirit of adoption (Rom. 8:14-18). Though
we suffer now, and 'groan within ourselves, waiting
eagerly for our adoption as sons' (waiting, that is, for
the consummation or completion of our adoption), yet
in the meantime the Spirit 'helps our weakness' by
interceding on our behalf (Rom. 8:23, 26). Thus we
pray with the total confidence and security of those
who are Christ's 'brethren' (Rom. 8:29), for whom all
things are working together for good (Rom. 8:28), who
cannot be separated from the love of Christ (Rom.
8:35ff), and who shall 'overwhelmingly conquer' in
Christ Jesus (Rom. 8:37).

If there is a fundamental instinct shared by all good
fathers it is that of protecting their children. A few
years back thousands of families fled Hurricane Floyd
with just that motivation – to protect their children.
Sometimes we parents are even *over*protective, trying
to shield our children from the hardships and
heartbreaks of the real world. That's how strong our
instinct to protect is. When our children are in danger,
they cry out to their daddies to protect them, confident
that they *can* and *will* do so. It is with this kind of
confidence that we cry out to God 'Our Father' in our

times of need. When we are afraid, when danger lurks, when enemies threaten we cry out to our Father with the confidence of His Fatherly protection and promise that 'no evil will befall (us)' (Ps. 91:10). We pray for protection from the safe haven of the 'shadow of the Almighty'. We have refuge 'under His wings'.

You will not be afraid of the terror by night, or of the arrow that flies by day; of the pestilence that stalks in darkness, or of the destruction that lays waste at noon. A thousand may fall at your side, and ten thousand at your right hand; but it shall not approach you (Ps. 91:5-7).

Do you have troubles? Do you have fears? Call upon your Father in heaven who promises to shield and protect us. 'Ten thousand' may fall at our right hand, but we are confident that as we pray for protection and safekeeping, our God extends His fatherly care and concern.

4. *We pray confident of the Father's provision.* We make requests to One who is eager to provide. This is the point of the concluding section of Matthew 6 (vv. 25-34), and the encouragement to prayer in 7:7-11. We are not to be anxious about what we are to eat, or drink, or with what we are to clothe ourselves, that is, about the basic necessities of life. Why not? Because God is our Father.

For all these things the Gentiles eagerly seek; for your heavenly Father knows that you need all these things (Matt. 6:32).

As was the case in 6:8, this knowing ('your heavenly Father knows') is not mere knowledge. He isn't just aware of the fact. The point is that He cares enough to know and take it into account. He 'knows' means He cares and will provide. This is the heavenly disposition that we encounter when we pray. We pray in the confidence that, as we ask, our Father will provide. Jesus encourages us in exactly this manner. He says:

> Ask, and it shall be given to you; seek, and you shall find; knock, and it shall be opened to you. For everyone who asks receives, and he who seeks finds, and to him who knocks it shall be opened (Matt. 7:7, 8).

How can we be sure of this? Because God is our Father. So Jesus reassures us:

> Or what man is there among you, when his son shall ask him for a loaf, will give him a stone? Or if he shall ask for a fish, he will not give him a snake, will he? If you then, being evil, know how to give good gifts to your children, how much more shall your Father who is in heaven give what is good to those who ask Him! (Matt. 7:9-11).

'How much more shall your Father who is in heaven give....' If the instinct to *protect* our children is fundamental to earthly fathers, closely associated with this is the instinct to *provide* as well. My grandfather worked twelve hours a day, six days a week, in the Pennsylvania coal mines from the 1920s to the 60s. During the winter he would go down the mine shaft in the dark and come out in the dark, and of course worked all day long in the dark. Only on Sunday did he see sunlight. He kept it up for fifty years and eventually died of black lung. I asked him once, 'Pop, why did you do it?' His answer was simple, 'I had to get bread on the table.' Fathers will endure almost anything to provide for their children. Today all over our nation parents are enduring enormous hardships, financial and otherwise, to provide what they deem to be a proper education for their children. Jesus is teaching us to see our God in this way as we pray. He provides for His children. We can count on His provision. We can count on His interest and concern as we cry out to Him for help. Go ahead, Peter says. 'Cast all your anxiety upon Him, because He cares for you' (1 Pet. 5:7). Similarly, Paul writes:

> Be anxious for nothing, but in everything by prayer and supplication with thanksgiving let your requests be made known to God (Phil. 4:6).

Our God is a loving Father to whom we can take our concerns and lay them at His feet. We can 'let (our) requests be made known to Him', with the confidence that He hears us as a father hears the pleas of his own children.

The *Westminster Confession of Faith* says that the sons of God, 'have access to the throne of grace with boldness, are enabled to cry, Abba, Father, are pitied, protected, provided for, and chastened by Him as by a Father, yet never cast off' (XII).

All this is implied by Jesus when He teaches us to pray, 'Our Father'. Consequently, we approach God now with 'boldness and confident access through faith in (Christ)' (Eph. 3:12). 'We have confidence to enter the holy place by the blood of Jesus, by a new and living way which He inaugurated for us' (Heb. 10:19ff).

4

Who Art in Heaven

The Father to whom we pray is our Father *in heaven*. This truth provides further critical perspective on how we pray and live. Because of our adoption in Christ, we pray with the total confidence, security, and acceptance that a child experiences in the lap of his father. Yet the Father whom we approach is not merely an earthly father with human limitations and corruptions, but a 'heavenly' Father (an adjective I mostly avoid due to its debasement in contemporary usage: heavenly dessert, heavenly hash, etc.), who is upon His throne in heaven. Jesus qualifies 'Our Father' with the words 'in heaven', not to indicate a limited location in which God alone is to be found. God is everywhere. 'Heaven and the highest heaven cannot contain Thee', says Solomon (1 Kgs. 8:27). Rather 'in heaven' is added in order to remind us of our Father's great dignity and power. 'Another way of saying the same thing', says Douglas Kelly, 'is that He is transcendent to everything. He is above all, He made all, and He is the source of all' (19). Jesus has already said:

'But I say to you, make no oath at all, either by heaven, for it is the throne of God' (Matt. 5:34).

'Heaven', He says, 'is the throne of God'. That is the point of 'in heaven'. We pray to a Father whose throne is *in heaven*. Heaven is mentioned because God rules from heaven. The Psalmist says:

> The Lord has established His throne in the heavens; and His sovereignty rules over all (Ps. 103:19).

The Lord says through Isaiah:

> 'Heaven is My throne, and the earth is My footstool' (Isa. 66:1a).

And again he says:

> For thus says the high and exalted One Who lives forever, whose name is Holy, 'I dwell on a high and holy place' (Isa. 57:15a).

A Reverent Prayer

If the mood of the Lord's Prayer is one of childlike confidence, the tone is one respectful of reverence. We may elaborate.

1. *We pray with respect for our Father's heavenly dignity.* Here too the human analogy helps: good fathers are both adored and feared. Their children both crawl into their laps with complete acceptance and comfort, *and* are careful not to cross them. Bad fathers are either feared and not adored, or adored and not feared. They are either too hard or too soft, too strict or too permissive. 'If I am a father, where is My honor?' God asks Israel (Mal. 1:6). Fathers, as such, are to be honored and revered. Our Father is 'lofty and exalted' (Isa. 6:1).

His throne is a 'glorious throne' (Matt. 19:28). Not only do we pray with the confidence that we are privileged, pitied, protected, and provided for, but also with the certainty that our God is a great God, and so is to be approached in prayer with 'reverence and awe' (Heb. 12:28). 'We should not miss the balance in this opening to the prayer', Morris warns us. 'We address God intimately as Father, but we immediately recognize His infinite greatness with the addition *in heaven*' (144). 'He is a Father, and therefore we may come to Him with boldness', says Matthew Henry, 'but a Father in heaven, and therefore we come with reverence'. Pink elaborates:

> What a blessed *balance* this gives to the previous phrase. If that tells us of God's goodness and grace, this speaks of His greatness and majesty. If that teaches us of the nearness and dearness of His relationship to us, this announces His infinite elevation above us. If the words 'Our Father' inspire confidence and love, then the words 'which art in heaven' should fill us with humility and awe. These are the two things that should ever occupy our minds and engage our hearts: the first without the second tends toward unholy familiarity; the second without the first produces coldness and dread. By combining them together, we are preserved from both evils; and a suitable equipoise is wrought and maintained in the soul as we duly contemplate both the mercy and might of God, His unfathomable love and His immeasurable loftiness (Pink, 80,81).

Our Father *in heaven,* then, points to the two sides of what we might call the 'psychology of adoption'. On the one hand I call upon God *grateful* for the privilege, *confident* because I am pitied and accepted, and *secure* because I am protected and provided for. Yet I also pray with *reverential fear* because our Father is *in heaven*.

Consequently we are to pray to our Father *respectfully*. Many of the older writers on prayer warn us of assuming an undue familiarity with the Almighty in our prayers, particularly on the part of those leading public services. 'Familiarity is the worst of faults in prayer', says W. G. T. Shedd (*Homiletics and Pastoral Theology*, 273). R. L. Dabney heaps scorn on 'Half-educated or spiritually proud men' who 'frequently indulge in an indecent familiarity with the Most High, under the pretence of filial nearness and importunity' (*Sacred Rhetoric or Courses of Lectures on Preaching,* 349). C. H. Spurgeon counsels that one avoid 'an unhallowed and sickening superabundance of endearing words'. He says, 'When 'Dear Lord' and 'Blessed Lord' and 'Sweet Lord', come over and over again as vain repetition, they are among the worst of blots'. He wishes that 'in some way or other', those who indulge such 'fond and familiar expressions', could come 'to a better understanding of the true relation existing between man and God' (*Lectures to My Students,* 57). He counsels that one be 'scrupulously reverent' in one's language (*Lectures,* 58). Those listening to our prayers should not conclude that we think that we have God in our hip-pocket.

Today we have the additional problem of *flippancy*. Whether motivated by the desire to startle or amuse, or just out of ignorance, some will refer to God as 'the Man upstairs', or worse, 'the Big Guy'. They will say, 'Hi God, it's me, Bob. How ya' doin?' 'Hey, I was just wonderin', and off they go. If the designation 'Father' invites intimacy with God, the addition of 'Heavenly' reminds us to avoid undue intimacy or flippancy, reminds us that God is in heaven, and we are on earth (Eccles. 5:1,2).

We also pray with *reverential fear*. Does reverence include 'fear'? Yes, properly understood it does. We are not to fear God with what the older writers called 'servile' fear. Godly fear is not terror. It is not fear inspired by iron justice or unpredictable, erratic, and disproportionate outbursts. We've all known of children who feared their fathers because they would be slapped down for the slightest offense, without any regard for mitigating circumstances. We are right to speak against such a view of God. It would be inconsistent with His character as Father. We do not speak to Him flinching, as some children do when addressing their fathers, frightened that at any moment they might strike them. As we've seen, God's basic orientation to us is that of sympathy. He is mindful of our weakness. Our fear, then, is not servile, but it is real fear.

Is this confusing to you? I am not surprised. Regrettably there is considerable teaching around today that takes the fact of our acceptance by God where the Bible doesn't take it. Some would insist that the implications of adoption eliminate the possibility of even reverential fear. The champions of this view will say such things as, 'God is *never* angry with His people'. Because we are saved by grace, they argue, He is never more or less pleased with us. He always sees us in Christ. Nothing I can do can make Him more happy with me. Nothing I can do can make Him less happy. I am complete in Christ. Whenever I come to Him He is completely pleased and satisfied with me. The problem with this, as I see it, is that while it may make good pop psychology, it is bad Biblical theology. Fundamentally, it fails to understand that God is my Father *in heaven*. Even earthly fathers are properly displeased with their earthly sons, aren't they? How much more so our holy Father in heaven. Do earthly sons fear the anger of their earthly fathers? Of course they do. Likewise the Bible teaches us to fear our heavenly Father's displeasure, while not failing to understand that it is the displeasure of our *Father*. Presumably all the New Testament writers understand their adoption in Christ. They all understand that God is their Father. Yet listen to them. Peter writes:

> And if you address as Father the One who impartially judges according to each man's work, conduct yourselves in fear during the time of your stay upon earth; knowing that you were not redeemed with perishable things like silver or gold from your futile way of life inherited from your forefathers, but with precious blood, as of a lamb unblemished and spotless, the blood of Christ (1 Pet. 1:17-19).

God is to be feared says Peter, not in spite of the fact that He is our Father, but because He is. 'If you address (Him) as *Father* ... conduct yourselves in *fear* ....' Peter tells us this in order to motivate us. Fear is a proper Christian motivation. Peter says to those suffering persecution:

> For it is time for judgment to begin with the household of God; and if it begins with us first, what will be the outcome for those who do not obey the gospel of God? (1 Pet. 4:17).

The household (*oikos*) is the family of God. Judgment begins there. Peter tells us this in order to give us perspective and motivate us. Our Father is evaluating our actions. We are judged in the same way that a good father assesses the activities of his children and approves or disapproves. Knowledge of His judgment is meant to provide incentive for Christian conduct and understanding of present suffering.

Listen to the progression in the Apostle Paul's thought:

> Therefore also we have as our ambition, whether at home or absent, to be pleasing to Him (2 Cor. 5:9).

What could it possibly mean to have as 'our ambition' to be 'pleasing' to God if He is never more or less pleased? It must mean that pleasing God is something that we are to strive to do, and displeasing Him, avoid. It must mean that at times my Father in heaven is displeased. Sometimes then I approach Him in prayer with the knowledge of His divine displeasure. Paul continues:

> For we must all appear before the judgment seat of Christ, that each one may be recompensed for his deeds in the body, according to what he has done, whether good or bad (2 Cor. 5:10).

Why does He refer to the 'judgment seat of Christ' unless it is to sober us with reverential fear? This is precisely what he says next:

> Therefore knowing the fear of the Lord, we persuade men, but we are made manifest to God; and I hope that we are made manifest also in your consciences (2 Cor. 5:11).

Why does he 'persuade men'? Because he knows the 'fear of the Lord'. Doesn't Paul know that he is loved and accepted? Doesn't he know that he is an adopted son of God? Of course he does, and he sees no conflict between reverential fear and sonship. In another place He says, even as a forgiven son of the living God:

> For if I preach the gospel, I have nothing to boast of, for I am under compulsion; for woe is me if I do not preach the gospel (1 Cor. 9:16).

What does he mean 'woe is me?' Does he fear God's displeasure? Does he fear God's judgment? Yes he does, and it motivates him. Listen to him again in that same chapter:

> Therefore I run in such a way, as not without aim; I box in such a way, as not beating the air; but I buffet my body and make it my slave, lest possibly, after I have preached to others, I myself should be disqualified (1 Cor. 9:26, 27).

He 'buffets' his body? He makes it his 'slave'? He fears that he might be 'disqualified'? Is this the language of a son? Of one who understands grace? Apparently so. Apparently God's acceptance of us in Christ by grace is not incompatible with an urgent avoidance of that which might 'disqualify' us from Christian service and perhaps heaven. He says this as one who is loved and secure, who is an adopted son, who is saved by grace and kept by grace.

Indeed, we can take this a step further. Not only is grace and adoption not incompatible with godly fear and urgency, it motivates urgency. It is *because* of 'the mercies of God' that we 'present our bodies as living sacrifices' (Rom. 12:1). Look at what Paul says in 1 Cor. 15:9, 10:

> For I am the least of the apostles, who am not fit to be called an apostle, because I persecuted the church of God. But by the grace of God I am what I am, and His grace toward me did not prove vain; but I labored even more than all of them, yet not I, but the grace of God with me.

We must add to the mixture of emotions that make up the psychology of adoption (and prayer) a profound sense of our unworthiness. Do you see it? 'I am ... not fit to be called an apostle', he says. Elsewhere he says, 'I am a nobody' (2 Cor. 12:11) and refers to himself as 'the very least of all the saints' (Eph. 3:8). He is keenly aware of his unworthiness and (as a result) of the greatness of God's grace to save him. Because of that grace he did what? 'I labored even more than all of them'. The one who is forgiven much loves (and serves) much! Grace motivates godly labor. But even here he adds that his hard work was enabled by God's grace: 'yet not I, but the grace of God with me'.

The point is that sometimes we will pray to our Father knowing that we are the objects of His displeasure and righteous anger. There are occasions when I come around the corner and catch my three-year-old with his hand in the cookie jar, and because he knows I am displeased and punishment is coming he'll come right over sobbing and hug my leg. He knows he's in trouble but he runs *to* me, sobbing and fearful! Sometimes we pray knowing that we've 'grieved' the Holy Spirit (Eph. 4:30). Is God never angry or displeased with His children? What then do we make of this grief? What do we make of the frequent mention of God's anger with his people in the Psalms (e.g. 37, 60, 77, 88, 90, 103)? The beloved Psalm 90 says:

> Lord, Thou hast been our dwelling place in all generations (Ps. 90:1).

That's all lovely and good. But it also goes on to say,

> For we have been consumed by Thine anger, and by Thy wrath we have been dismayed. Thou hast placed our iniquities before Thee, our secret sins in the light of Thy presence. For all our days have declined in Thy fury; we have finished our years like a sigh. As for the days of our life, they contain seventy years, Or if due to strength, eighty years, yet their pride is but labor and sorrow; for soon it is gone and we fly away. Who understands the power of Thine anger, and Thy fury, according to the fear that is due Thee? So teach us to number our days, that we may present to Thee a heart of wisdom (Ps. 90:7-12).

Wrath, anger, fury, fear — they are all there. Or look at Psalm 103. The same Psalm that says that the Lord pities us as a father pities his children states, 'He will not keep His anger forever' (v. 9). Are we to believe that God was angry with only His Old Testament people and not with those of the New Testament? That would seem to be the opposite of what the Apostle Paul would have us conclude in 1 Cor. 10, where he describes the Exodus and wilderness generations as 'laid low' because God 'was not well pleased' (1 Cor. 10:5). And the point?:

Now these things happened as examples for us, that
we should not crave evil things, as they also craved
... Now these things happened to them as an
example, and they were written for our instruction,
upon whom the ends of the ages have come (1 Cor.
10:6, 11).

How are we to make sense of all this? As the writer to
the Hebrews does: as the chastening hand of a displeased
and righteous Father. The Fatherhood of God is the
key. Our adoptive sonship provides the perspective:

and you have forgotten the exhortation which is
addressed to you as sons, My son, do not regard
lightly the discipline of the Lord, nor faint when
you are reproved by Him; for those whom the Lord
loves He disciplines, and He scourges every son
whom He receives. It is for discipline that you
endure; God deals with you as with sons; for what
son is there whom his father does not discipline?
But if you are without discipline, of which all have
become partakers, then you are illegitimate
children and not sons. Furthermore, we had earthly
fathers to discipline us, and we respected them; shall
we not much rather be subject to the Father of
spirits, and live? For they disciplined us for a short
time as seemed best to them, but He disciplines us
for our good, that we may share His holiness. All
discipline for the moment seems not to be joyful,
but sorrowful; yet to those who have been trained
by it, afterwards it yields the peaceful fruit of
righteousness (Heb. 12:5-11).

'Fatherly love on the one hand and transcendent
greatness on the other, are the two qualities in God
which the rest of the prayer assumes at every point',

says Packer (135). Consequently when I come to God in prayer, I come to my righteous and holy Father in heaven. He is *my* Father, and therefore I am secure. But security is not presumption. He is also a holy and heavenly Father, and therefore I am eager to please Him, grieving whenever I fail to do so. I know the comfort of His staff and the sting of His rod (Ps. 23). I am zealous to please and yet fear His wrath. I relate to God as I relate to a good Father, confident of His unchanging love, fearing His reproof, and grieving over what the *Westminster Confession of Faith* calls His 'Fatherly displeasure'.

2. *We pray with childlike trust in our Father's power and goodness.* We may have already made this point, but perhaps it needs a further moment of emphasis. There are bad fathers. There are mediocre fathers. There are good fathers, yet even in them there is significant corruption and failure. Some have been so alarmed by the failure of human fathers, and the damage done to those who have been their victims, that they have been ready to jettison the category of fatherhood altogether. But when Jesus selected the title of 'Father', He did so knowing that all human fathers are flawed and provide a distorted reflection of God's Fatherhood. Yet because we learn by both positive and negative examples ('I want to be like that' ... 'I'll never treat my children like he does,' etc.) we are able to envision the ideal Fatherhood to which our corrupt examples point. Our earthly fathers fall and fail, they disappoint and discourage. Often they mean well but are weak. They would like to help us but lack the ability. But our heavenly Father can be trusted. He is *able* and *willing* to help. Consequently, as I begin to lay my burdens before

Him, I do so with the confidence that He not only cares, but is able to resolve my problems. We have seen that we are pitied, protected, and provided for by our Father. Now we need merely to underscore the blessed fact that He is able to provide the things of which we have need. 'Nothing is too difficult for Him' (Jer. 32:17). With God, 'all things are possible' (Matt. 19:26; cf Luke 1:37). 'He does according to His will in the hosts of heaven and among the inhabitants of earth; and no one can ward off His hand or say to Him "what hast Thou done?"' (Dan. 4:35). Do you have friends and relatives who are 'incredibly unsaved', as one of our former members once put it. 'He is able to save unto the uttermost', says the writer to the Hebrews (Heb. 7:25). He is able to change the heart of the most hardened and hateful rebel.

Do you have problems in your family? Is your marriage unstable? Are the children in trouble? Your Father in heaven is able to do 'exceeding abundantly' beyond all we could ask or think (Eph. 3:20). He is able and willing to restore love and tenderness to your marriage. He is able and willing to deliver your children from worldly and destructive influences. Ask!

Do we have needs in our church? Do we lack funds? He owns 'the cattle on a thousand hills' (Ps. 50:10). Do we lack unity? Our Father is able and willing to root and ground us in love (Eph. 3:17). He is able to give us the same mind, the same love, one spirit and one purpose (Phil. 2:2). Do we lack fruitfulness in our ministry? Why does Paul pray that we should be 'bearing fruit in all respects' unless God could hear and answer that prayer (Col. 1:9ff)? Why would Jesus teach us to 'beseech the Lord of the harvest to send out workers into His harvest' unless by so praying, the

Father will respond by raising up ministers and missionaries (Matt. 9:36-38)? Why does He pray, 'that God may open up to us a door for the word', unless doors of opportunity swing open as we pray for them? Likewise, we speak as we ought when we ask for help in doing so. Paul says, 'pray ... that I may make it clear in the way I ought to speak' (Col. 4:2-4). Do you lack spiritual maturity, understanding, and wisdom? Look at how often the Apostle Paul prays for these things for believers (Eph. 1:15-23, 3:14-19; Phil. 1:9-11; Col. 1:9-11). Why would he do so unless our heavenly Father were willing and able to grant these requests?

Jesus invites us to pray to One who is both able and willing to help because He is our Father. We come to Him with our prayers, not like a bratty child, demanding and ordering Him about, whining and fussing whenever He does not do exactly what we want when we request it. We come not like a fresh child, flippant and disrespectful, behaving as though God were in our hip pocket, our 'personal God' who goes along with our personal computers, who exists merely to meet our needs. No, 'our' identifies us as belonging to a community of believers with whom and for whom we pray. 'Our Father' identifies us as believers who are grateful, confident, and secure in the privilege of sonship, and the pity, protection, and provision that goes with it. 'Our Father who art in heaven' identifies us as believers whose boldness is tempered by respect, reverence, and godly fear. Sinclair Ferguson summarizes the Biblical balance in these words:

'We do not live in intimacy with God in a way that destroys our reverence for Him or in a manner that isolates us from our fellow Christians' (162).

III

The Petitions

5

The Petitions

Larger Catechism #189:

> Q. *What doth the preface of the Lord's Prayer teach us?*
> A. The preface of the Lord's Prayer (contained in these words, *Our Father which art in heaven),* teacheth us, when we pray, to draw near to God with confidence of his fatherly goodness, and our interest therein; with reverence, and all other childlike dispositions, heavenly affections, and due apprehensions of his sovereign power, majesty, and gracious condescension: and also, to pray with and for others.

The catechism wisely summarizes that which we have seen: we come to our God in prayer with 'confidence of His fatherly goodness' and 'all other childlike dispositions', for He is 'our Father', *ours* together as the people of God, ours by adoption. We pray then with all the security, acceptance, confidence, and boldness of beloved children approaching their adored Father. We also approach Him with 'reverence', with 'due apprehensions of His sovereign power, majesty and gracious condescension', with respect and godly fear, for He is our Father *in heaven.* We are comfortable, comforted, and safe in His presence. Yet we also bring to our prayers reverential awe of His majesty, tears of sorrow when we have displeased Him, and a healthy fear (not terror) of His discipline. We pray as 'beloved children' (Eph. 5:1) yet to a 'holy Father' (John 17:11). These are the two sides of Christian experience, and it is important that we do not allow one to cancel out the other. Security and acceptance should not overshadow reverence and godly fear, lest we become complacent about our conduct and presumptuous about His grace. Reverence and godly fear should not overshadow security and acceptance, lest we live in dread of God and are unable to enjoy His presence or believe His promises.

Given that the Lord's Prayer may serve as a *pattern* or *outline* for our prayers (public and private) and that each word is but a heading that is 'concise and yet vastly comprehensive', as Henry says in his *Method*, we might elaborate or 'dialate (*sic*) upon the several passages and petitions of it'. We might pray 'Our Father' in the following manner:

'We come to You, our Father, as your children, saved by Your mercy and grace, adopted in Christ Jesus into Your family, members of your household (1 Pet. 4:17), and enjoying all the privileges of the children of God (John 1:12). We rejoice that you have predestined us to adoption as sons in Christ Jesus (Eph. 1:5). In the fullness of time You sent Your Son to redeem us that we might become your children (Gal. 4:5). We come to you no longer as slaves or orphans but as sons and heirs (John 14:18; Gal. 4:6,7). We are Your body (1 Cor. 12:12ff). We are Your temple (2 Cor. 6:16). We are Your people. We are Your bride, whom you love, and nourish, and cherish (Eph. 5:22ff). We are your family and we come to you as brothers and sisters in Christ. We rejoice that You love and pity us, even as a father pities his children (Ps. 103:13). We rest secure in Your strong protection. We find fatherly refuge in You (Prov. 14:26). No one shall pluck us from Your hand (John 10:28). We are kept by Your power (1 Pet. 1:5). You are for us a Father who knows our needs even before we ask (Matt. 6:25-34). You are a Father who gives good gifts to His children (Matt. 7:9-11). And so we come to You boldly and securely in Christ, confident to enter the holy place by the blood of Jesus, by a new and living way which He inaugurated for us (Eph. 3:12; Heb. 10:19). We come knowing that we are pitied, provided for, and protected; knowing that You our Father are working all things together for our good, that none can separate us from Your love, that in Christ we overwhelmingly conquer (Rom. 8:28ff).'

We prayerfully rehearse the things we know, and about which we are sure, as sons of our Father. Why? Two reasons. First, this is what pleases our Father. He delights in hearing us review in prayer the things that He has revealed about Himself. Second, by this we *strengthen* our faith. By *reminding* ourselves of who He is and who we are in relation to Him (and in so doing thanking and praising God for His good gifts). This reinforces our convictions so that we are able to pray with faith. How much time do we spend doing these things? Long enough to stimulate and deepen our faith. We might continue our prayer in this way as we remind ourselves that He is our Father *in heaven*:

'Our Father, we come to give to You the honor which a Father deserves (Mal. 1:6). You are lofty and exalted (Is 6:1). Heaven is Your throne, earth is Your footstool (Isa. 66:1). Heaven and highest heaven cannot contain You (1 Kgs. 8:27). You have established your throne in the heavens, and your sovereignty rules over all (Ps. 103:19). Nothing is too difficult for You (Jer. 32:17). For You all things are possible (Matt. 19:26). Nothing is impossible for You (Luke 1:37). You do Your will in the hosts of heaven and among the inhabitants of earth. No one can ward off Your hand or say to You, 'What have You done?' (Dan. 4:35). You dwell in a high and holy place, and also with the contrite and lowly of spirit (Isa. 57:15). We lift our eyes to You, O You who are enthroned in the heavens (Ps. 123:1). Look down from heaven, and see from Your holy and glorious habitation (Isa. 63:15)'.

We pray in this way not merely because we have been given a formula by Jesus by which we are to pray. Rather we pray in this way because these are our deepest convictions. Our prayers flow naturally from us and are an expression of our way of living. We are not 'anxious' about life and death. We live lives of faith, peace, and joy. We are confident that He will favorably hear our requests and give good gifts. Why? Because God is *our Father*. We are not morally sloppy or carnal or flippant about the things of God, but live careful, sober, serious, and intentional lives. Why? Because God is our Father *in heaven*. Thus we have addressed Him as *Our Father in Heaven:* our *Father* by whom we are accepted, with whom we have confidence, and in whom we are secure; and our Father in *heaven* to whom we show respect, reverence, and godly fear. This is both the *mood* and *tone* of our prayer.

Petitions

Now we may begin to look at the petitions. As noted earlier, Jesus uses six petitions in the Lord's Prayer: three respecting God and three respecting ourselves. With which petitions does Jesus begin? With those having to do with God:

1. Hallowed be Thy name
2. Thy kingdom come
3. Thy will be done

The last petition concludes with the clause, 'on earth, as it is in heaven'. R T. France suggests that it applies to all three petitions: that God's name be hallowed on earth as it is in heaven, His kingdom come on earth as it is in heaven, and that His will be done on earth as it is in heaven. This gives to the petitions an eschatological dimension. In our prayers we long to see on earth that which can only be consummated when Christ returns. In a sense, the petitions are three parallel requests, almost three requests for the same thing. They are three ways of asking that God receive the honor that He deserves.

God First

Notice that all this comes before any attention is given to our personal needs. Before I ask for anything for myself or ourselves, I am to pray for God's name, kingdom and will. God comes first, I come second. As Calvin and Matthew Henry observe, this parallels the Ten Commandments, where our duties are divided into two categories: first, our duty toward God (commands 1-4); second, duty to man (commands 5-10). Another way of saying this is that the praise of God precedes personal petitions. 'Praise', or concern for God's affairs, comes first. Matthew Henry says:

> Let Him have the praise of His perfections, and then let us have the benefit of them.

The implications of this method of prayer take us far beyond prayer and into a whole way of life. A disciple of Christ is one who prays for God's name, kingdom, and will even before he asks for bread! Why does he do this? Let us say it again and again. Because this is how he lives. For us to pray this way we must first begin to live this way. For us to live this way a Copernican Revolution must take place in our hearts, taking us out of the center of our universe and placing God there instead. The praying disciple of Christ has first in his heart and first on his lips the kingdom and glory of Christ. This is his great concern. This is his passion. His own concerns and needs, his personal agenda, all take a back seat to God's. *Our theology of prayer is our theology of Christian living.* Why does the disciple of Christ begin his prayer with God? Because his chief end in prayer, as well as all of life, is the glory of God. His concern is that, 'in all things God may be glorified through Jesus Christ' (1 Pet. 4:11). As for himself, he is not his own (1 Cor. 6:19). He, along with his own needs, wants, dreams, and aspirations, was crucified with Christ. He no longer lives (Gal. 2:20). He has taken up his cross. He's lost his life (Matt. 16:24-26). He is no longer living for himself but for Christ (2 Cor. 5:15). His attitude is that of John the Baptist, who was enjoying a 'successful' ministry. '*All* the country of Judea was going out to him, and *all* the people of Jerusalem' (Mark 1:5). Yet when his disciples began to complain that all the crowds were following Jesus and no longer following John, he responded not with bitterness or jealousy. Instead he said, 'He must increase, but I must decrease' (John 3:30). This is the motto of the Christian. This is our theme for life: 'He must increase, but I must decrease'.

The order of the petitions reminds us of our greatest challenge. For many the problem is not so much selfishness; they are generous and sympathetic to a fault. It is self-*centeredness*. Packer reminds us, 'Were we left to ourselves, any praying that we do would both start and end with ourselves, for our natural self-centeredness knows no bounds' (144). Am I at the center of all things and does all else revolve around me? Or is God at the center? The order of the Lord's Prayer shapes the order for our lives. God, His name, kingdom, and will are first. I, with my needs, wants, and desires, am second.

Model Prayers

Moreover, this is what we see throughout the Bible. When the people of God pray, this is how they pray. They pray 'God first, me second'. They first acknowledge, praise, and thank God, and only then do they move on to petitions. Let us provide several examples. Listen to David's great prayer on the occasion of the dedication of the materials to be used in the construction of the temple:

> So David blessed the Lord in the sight of all the assembly; and David said, 'Blessed art Thou, O Lord God of Israel our father, forever and ever. Thine, O Lord, is the greatness and the power and the glory and the victory and the majesty, indeed everything that is in the heavens and the earth;

Thine is the dominion, O Lord, and Thou dost exalt Thyself as head over all. Both riches and honor come from Thee, and Thou dost rule over all, and in Thy hand is power and might; and it lies in Thy hand to make great, and to strengthen everyone. Now therefore, our God, we thank Thee, and praise Thy glorious name' (1 Chron. 29:10-13).

David piles up one praiseworthy attribute after another. Not until verses 18 and 19 does he finally get around to petitions: preserve the good intentions of the people, give Solomon a heart to keep the commandments, and build the temple. Even as kingdom-oriented as these petitions are, they come second, well behind the praise and thanks of God.

King Hezekiah, at a time of supreme crisis, with Jerusalem surrounded by the Assyrian hosts, prayed:

O Lord, the God of Israel, who art enthroned above the cherubim, Thou art the God, Thou alone, of all the kingdoms of the earth. Thou hast made heaven and earth (2 Kgs. 19:15).

In spite of the calamity about to befall the city, only after praising God does he turn to petitions.

Incline Thine ear, O Lord, and hear; open Thine eyes, O Lord, and see; and listen to the words of Sennacherib, which he has sent to reproach the living God.... And now, O Lord our God, I pray, deliver us from his hand that all the kingdoms of the earth may know that Thou alone, O Lord, art God' (2 Kgs. 19:16, 19).

The praise and glory of God come first. Only after this do petitions follow. Jeremiah provides us with another example. Having been told that he must buy land in a Jerusalem about to be taken captive by the Babylonians (making such a purchase nonsensical) he prays:

> Ah Lord God! Behold, Thou hast made the heavens and the earth by Thy great power and by Thine outstretched arm! Nothing is too difficult for Thee, who showest lovingkindness to thousands, but repayest the iniquity of fathers into the bosom of their children after them, O great and mighty God. The Lord of hosts is His name; great in counsel and mighty in deed, whose eyes are open to all the ways of the sons of men, giving to everyone according to his ways and according to the fruit of his deeds (Jer. 32:17-19).

Only in verse 25 does he finally get around to his issue, 'And Thou hast said to me, O Lord God, "Buy for yourself the field with money, and call in witnesses" – although the city is given into the hand of the Chaldeans'. God is first. Jeremiah's need or interest is second.

This, you see, is the Biblical way. The saints of old and the saints today all live and pray with God at the center. Do you wish to make progress in the Christian life? This is the first step, in life and in prayer. Seek first the kingdom of God and His righteousness (Matt. 6:33). 'Do all to the glory of God' (1 Cor. 10:31). Our chief end, says the *Shorter Catechism*, is 'to glorify God and to enjoy Him forever'. Prayer, as Packer puts it, is not an attempt on our part 'to bend God's will to our own', but rather is 'a means to our Father's glory' (135).

The first lesson of the Lord's Prayer, he maintains, 'is to grasp that God matters infinitely more than we do' (144). Or in Pink's words, 'our primary duty in prayer is to disregard ourselves and to give God the pre-eminence in our thoughts, desires, and supplications' (83).

6

Hallowed Be Thy Name

Let us remember the structure of Jesus' model prayer up to this point.

Preface – Our Father Who Art in Heaven (6:9)

Petitions –
For God's glory – Hallowed be Thy Name. Thy kingdom come. Thy will be done, on earth as it is in heaven (Matt. 6:10).
For our needs – Give us this day our daily bread. And forgive us our debts, as we also have forgiven our debtors. And do not lead us into temptation, but deliver us from evil. [For Thine is the kingdom, and the power, and the glory, forever. Amen] (Matt. 6:11-13).

As we have seen, the order is significant. Only after we have offered our praise to God and pled for the glory of His name, kingdom, and will, do we give attention to our own needs. Thus in prayer, as in all of life, we are to seek first the kingdom of God (Matt. 6:33). This point was developed extensively in Section 4, and does not need to be repeated again except to underscore it. If there is one lesson to be learned from the Lord's Prayer to this point it is this: we are to be *God-centered* in our praying and living. Jesus is teaching a God-centered piety.

The first petition that Jesus teaches us to pray is, 'Hallowed be Thy name'. Above all else the name of God is in our hearts and on our lips. What does it mean? To 'hallow' the name of God means literally 'to sanctify', meaning to 'treat as holy, reverence' (Arndt and Gingrich, *Greek-English Lexion*, 2nd ed.). It is to pray that God's name will be 'held in proper reverence' (Morris, 145); that its sanctity will be recognized or considered, even that it will be 'treated as holy' (Carson, 170); that it will be 'known, acknowledged and honored as holy' (Packer, 144).

God's Name
The 'name' of God is more than a personal designation or label, as names tend to be for us. The 'name' is the person and the qualities that make up the person. To praise the name of God is to praise His person, or simply, to praise Him. 'God's "name" is God Himself as He is and has revealed Himself', says Carson (170). His name designates 'all that God is and stands for', says Morris (145); it 'stands for the divine perfections', adds Pink, and 'sets before us all that God has revealed to us concerning Himself' (84, 85).

Several examples will illustrate this meaning. The angel told Joseph that the Messiah's *name* shall be 'Jesus' because 'he shall save his people from their sins' (Matt. 1:21). The name signifies the One *and* His work. 'Those who know Thy name (i.e. know who You are, know what You are like) will put their trust in Thee' (Ps. 9:10). 'We will boast in the name (i.e. the person that

He is) of the Lord our God' (Ps. 20:7). Jesus prays, 'Father, glorify Thy name' (John 12:28), that is, glorify *Yourself*. To pray that God's name should be hallowed is to pray that He will get the honor, the respect, the reverence, the fear, the glory of which He is worthy. His name is hallowed because His is an 'honored and awesome name' (Deut. 28:58). His is 'the name which is above every name' (Phil. 2:9).

God's Honor

This then is our first petition. Our first concern is that God's name would be hallowed 'on earth, even as it is in heaven'. The first petition signifies our desire 'that God's matchless name might be reverenced, adored, and glorified, and that God might cause it to be held in the utmost respect and honor, that its fame might spread abroad and be magnified', (Pink, 84). When will that happen? Finally and completely only when Christ returns. But in the meantime, it happens gradually and incrementally as more and more people and nations are won to Christ. Why would we pray this way? Because of our passion to see God honored. We long to hasten the day when *at the name of Jesus* every knee shall bow and every tongue confess (Phil. 2:10,11); when the knowledge of the glory of God will cover the earth as the water covers the seas (Hab. 2:14); when no man shall teach his brother saying 'know the Lord,' for each man shall know Him from the least to the greatest (Jer. 31:34; Heb. 8:11). We long to see God get His glory, for His glory to be recognized, for the peoples of the world to unite in praising our God. This is the vision of the Psalms. Listen to what we sing (the following Psalms are given in their metrical versions as found in the *Trinity Psalter*):

All peoples, clap your hands for joy;
To God in triumph shout;
For awesome is the LORD Most High,
Great King the earth throughout.

He brings the peoples under us
In mastery complete;
And He it is Who nations all
Subdues beneath our feet (Ps. 47:1-3).

All lands to God in joyful sounds
Aloft your voices raise;
Sing forth the honor of His name,
And glorious make His praise,
And glorious make His praise (Ps. 66:1, 2).

All people that on earth do dwell,
Sing to the Lord with cheerful voice,
Him serve with mirth; His praise forth tell;
Come ye before Him and rejoice.

(Ps. 100:1, 2; cf Pss. 22, 67, 72)

Abhorrence of Evil

'All nations', 'all lands', and 'all people' are to sing to
the praise of God. In this we rejoice. Likewise, we
experience the opposite: grief and sorrow when His
name is desecrated, dishonored, or blasphemed. Thus
was the spirit of the Apostle Paul 'provoked within
him as he was beholding the city full of idols' (Acts
17:16). The word 'provoked' (*paroxunoo*) has a range
of meanings from enrage, to irritate, to grieve, to
exasperate. Paul was *deeply disturbed* by the sight of
the idols of Athens. When he looked out at that noted
city, that home of the arts and letters, that home of the
Parthenon, of Socrates, of Plato, that 'Cradle of

Democracy', he saw not its unsurpassed culture, but its idolatry, and was profoundly troubled. He was 'provoked', He was zealous to proclaim the gospel to them. This is why we pray in this way. Like Paul, we are 'jealous ... with a godly jealousy' for God's glory (2 Cor. 11:2). Like Elijah, we are 'very jealous for the Lord, the God of hosts' (1 Kgs. 19:10).

'Hallowed be Thy name' heads our petitions because God's glory is supreme among all of our desires, and conversely, because we cannot bear to see God dishonored. We grieve that our countrymen are 'lovers of self, lovers of money', and 'lovers of pleasure rather than lovers of God' (2 Tim. 3:2, 4). We are deeply troubled that we are a people 'whose god is their belly' (Phil. 3:19). When we see God dishonored, disregarded, and disobeyed in our mass media, in our schools and universities, on our sports fields and in our arenas, on our streets and in our clinics, we cry out 'hallowed be Thy name'. We cannot be indifferent to these things. They trouble us, and in so doing provoke us to prayer and outreach, that multitudes will be saved and God will get His glory.

Paul says that we are to 'abhor what is evil and cling to what is good' (Rom. 12:9). We are not passively indifferent. We do not flirt with sin. We *abhor* it. We do not 'rejoice in unrighteousness, but rejoice with the truth' (1 Cor. 13:6). We cannot bear to see idolatry and immorality and injustice advance. We cannot bear to see God's name being trampled in the dust. Zeal for our Father's house consumes us as it did Jesus (Ps. 69:9). This is why we pray 'hallowed be Thy name'. O that God would get His glory! 'Not to us, O Lord, not to us, but to Thy name give glory' (Ps. 115:1). This is our first concern. This is our first motive in evangelism, and our first petition in prayer. The *Larger Catechism* puts it this way:

> Q. 190 *What do we pray for in the first petition?*
> A. In the first petition (which is, *Hallowed be thy name),* acknowledging the utter inability and indisposition that is in ourselves and all men to honor God aright, we pray, that God would by his grace enable and incline us and others to know, to acknowledge, and highly to esteem him, his titles, attributes, ordinances, Word, works, and whatsoever he is pleased to make himself known by; and to glorify him in thought, word, and deed: that he would prevent and remove atheism, ignorance, idolatry, profaneness, and whatsoever is dishonorable to him; and by his overruling providence, direct and dispose of all things to his own glory.

Care for His Name

For us to pray this prayer and mean it we will need to begin to take care how we personally and collectively use the name of God. We are never to allow His name to be used in a 'vain' or empty or frivolous manner (Exod. 20:3). Do not allow it to become a punctuation mark in your conversations, as in 'Oh my _____'. Do not allow it to be invoked in profane swearing, as in when God is called upon to damn someone. Amazingly the name Jesus Christ itself is frequently used as a curse. Never, ever should His name be used in this way. Neither should we use the euphemisms which encourage us to get close to blasphemy without crossing the line. 'Egad' and 'oh my gosh' and 'Jiminy Cricket' and 'Geeze'. The 'G' words and 'J' words all come close! Because one can be mistakenly heard as saying the divine name itself, it is best to avoid all such words altogether.

Reverent Worship

We also hallow the name of God when we pray and worship God reverently. We are commanded to worship God with 'reverence and awe' (Heb. 12:28). The *Westminster Confession of Faith* outlines three settings in which God is to be worshiped: in *private*, in *families*, and in *public*.[1] We honor God when we reverently sing His praise, read and expound His word, and offer our prayers in the closet, the home, and in the church. Care should be taken to think and express great thoughts of God.

It is possible, we may deduce, to sing, pray, teach, read and listen, vow, give and receive the sacraments irreverently. When have we crossed the line separating reverence from irreverence? We would have to judge that on a case-by-case basis. But our goal ought not to be to see how close we can get to the line without crossing over, but to avoid getting anywhere near it. At the *name* of Jesus knees *bow* (Phil. 2:10). That gives us some idea of how we are to hallow the name of God in prayer and worship. What is in our hearts and on our lips must be compatible with the posture of bowing. Listen to the Apostle Paul as he prays:

> For this reason, I bow my knees before the Father, from whom every family in heaven and on earth derives its name (Eph. 3:14,15).

Paul prays and he bows.

The prayers and worship of heaven also provide us with a clue regarding reverence. We read:

> And when the living creatures give glory and honor and thanks to Him who sits on the throne, to Him

---

[1] See *The Family Worship Book*, 1-47

who lives forever and ever, the twenty-four elders will fall down before Him who sits on the throne, and will worship Him who lives forever and ever, and will cast their crowns before the throne, saying, 'Worthy art Thou, our Lord and our God, to receive glory and honor and power; for Thou didst create all things, and because of Thy will they existed, and were created' (Rev. 4:9-11).

As the twenty-four elders worship, they 'fall down'. Prostration accompanies the praise of heaven (cf 5:14). In practical terms, this means that we can never pray at home or worship in church in a light, casual, flippant, or frivolous manner. There ought always to be a seriousness, a sobriety, an earnestness, a solemnity about our private prayer and our public worship. Thus do we hallow, thus do we honor and respect the name of our God. We ought not to 'lighten-up' in worship any more than we lighten-up for baptisms, weddings, and funerals. When we deal with ultimate realities including all our dealings with God, we ought to do so with seriousness and respect.

Our 'chief end', we remind ourselves again, 'is to glorify God and to enjoy Him forever'. The hallowing and glorifying of God's name is both *duty* and *delight*. While it is serious business it is not drudgery. As we glorify God we enjoy Him. 'He has so made us', says Packer, 'that we find our deepest fulfillment and highest joy in hallowing his name' (147).

7

Thy Kingdom Come

The second petition is, 'Thy kingdom come'. A. W. Pink makes the valuable observation that whereas the first petition, 'Hallowed be Thy name' has to do with the honoring of God, or God's glory itself, the second and third petitions have to do with the means to that end. 'God's name is manifestly glorified here only in the proportion in which His *kingdom* comes to us and His *will* is done by us', he affirms (91). We are praying in this petition and the next for the means by which God's name will be hallowed.

The Kingdom of God is a prominent theme in the New Testament. What does it mean? The *kingdom* of God means simply the *rule* of God. It is 'his royal rule', says Stott (147). Where is it? It is present wherever the rule of Christ has been established. 'He is said to be *reigning* over men', says Calvin, 'when they subdue their flesh to His yoke, and their own desires are laid aside, so they willingly bind and give themselves over to His rule' (207). 'It exists wherever men enthrone Jesus as master of their lives', says Packer (149). Thus we encounter once more the 'already' and the 'not yet'. The kingdom of God was announced in the preaching of Jesus and is present in His person. He began His preaching, as John the Baptist had begun his.

From that time Jesus began to preach and say, 'Repent, for the kingdom of heaven is at hand' (Matt. 4:17; cf. Matt. 3:2).

Likewise Jesus sent out the disciples saying:

And as you go, preach, saying, 'The kingdom of heaven is at hand' (Matt. 10:7).

Jesus could even say:

For behold, the kingdom of God is in your midst (Luke 17:21b).

The kingdom, God's rule, was 'at hand' or 'in your midst' because Jesus was present manifesting the kingdom of God through teaching, casting out demons, and healing. Similarly today the kingdom or rule of God is present whenever and wherever Christ is believed and obeyed. It is present *now*, 'already' in so far as Jesus is believed and obeyed *now*. It lies in the *future*, it is 'not yet' in that it is partial or incomplete and awaits consummation. Listen to the Apostle Paul discussing the resurrection on the last day:

For as in Adam all die, so also in Christ all shall be made alive. But each in his own order: Christ the first fruits, after that those who are Christ's at His coming, then comes the end, when He delivers up the kingdom to the God and Father, when He has abolished all rule and all authority and power. For He must reign until He has put all His enemies under His feet. The last enemy that will be abolished is death (1 Cor. 15:22-26; cf 1 Cor. 4:20).

Jesus now reigns: 'For He must reign *until* ....' That is, He now is reigning and must continue to reign 'until' the end. But that reign, in the meantime, is partial and awaits consummation: '... until He has put all His enemies under His feet'. Then He will hand over to His Father the consummated kingdom, 'when He delivers up the kingdom to the God and Father' (v. 24). Paul goes on to define the consummated kingdom as that place where 'All things are put in subjection' (1 Cor. 15:27-28). The kingdom is Christ's rule, partial now, completed then. Now 'we do not yet see all things subjected to Him' (Heb. 2:8). Both of these passages (1 Cor. 15, Heb. 2) cite Psalm 8 ('He has put all things in subjection under His feet') as prophesying of Christ's kingdom. The kingdom is not now complete in that all things are not yet subject to Christ. Yet one day they shall be.

This prayer then is twofold: that Christ's rule will be extended more and more *now*, and that Christ will come and complete His rule upon His return *then*. Our prayer is that more and more men and nations will recognize the sovereignty of Christ and surrender to His rule. We may elaborate in this way.

Kingdom of Grace
First, we are praying that God's kingdom of grace will come. Jesus' kingdom is 'not of this world' (John 18:36). It is a spiritual kingdom, a kingdom of grace. Consequently it is not extended or advanced by the methods by which earthly kingdoms are. Jesus said if it were, 'my servants would be fighting'. Christ does not use armies, navies, laws, ballot boxes, entertainment, or money. Why? Because He is primarily concerned with establishing His kingdom

in human hearts. 'We do not war according to the flesh', says the Apostle. His kingdom advances one changed life at a time. 'The weapons of our warfare are not of the flesh, but divinely powerful for the destruction of fortresses ... and every lofty thing raised up against the knowledge of God' (2 Cor. 10:3-6). We put on the 'full armor of God', not the steel armor of man, because:

> Our struggle is not against flesh and blood, but against the rulers, against the powers, against the world forces of this darkness, against the spiritual forces of wickedness in the heavenly places (Eph. 6:12).

How does this kingdom come? It comes as we wield the spiritual weapons of the word, sacraments, and prayer in the context of godliness, love, and good works. Christ has given the church the 'keys of the kingdom of heaven' and the power of 'binding' (or forbidding) and loosing (or permitting) (Matt. 16:19). The keys open the doors of heaven. Our prayers turn the key! When we pray for the coming of the kingdom, we are asking that God would subdue and conquer our neighbors, our friends, our nation, the world; that the masses of the people will come to Christ; that a multitude that no-one can number will be won. 'Thy kingdom come' is a prayer that the world will surrender, submit to, bow before the Lord Jesus Christ.

Among the earliest of Christian confessions is, 'Jesus is Lord'. One of the many ironies of our day is that the language of conversion which is in the Bible is at times exchanged by preachers and others for language that is not. For example, we sometimes mistakenly urge people to 'accept' Jesus Christ. This is a weak, and I must say defective, way of formulating what it means to become a Christian. Our interpersonal parallels make this obvious. We say of Mr So and So, 'He just wants acceptance. He just wants to be accepted by you'. Mr So and So is cast into the role of victim by the language of acceptance. Poor fellow. He just wants to belong, to be one of the gang. It goes without saying, I trust, that such is inadequate terminology for conversion to Christ. Jesus is not passively seeking acceptance. He is not pleading that we let Him be a part of our lives. He does not have a psychological need for a place at our table. He does not need us at all. Rather He is actively demanding and commanding submission. This is how Peter preached at Pentecost. Jesus has been 'exalted to the right hand of God' (Acts 2:33). His enemies are being made a 'footstool' for his feet (Acts 2:34, 35, citing Ps. 110:1 this time).

> Therefore let all the house of Israel know for certain that God has made Him both Lord and Christ – this Jesus whom you crucified (Acts 2:36).

He is Lord. He is Messiah (i.e. the Davidic King!). How then were they to respond? 'Repent and let each of you be baptized in the name of Jesus Christ' (Acts 2:38). His Lordship commands the submission of repentance. That is, the submission of repudiating all that God calls sin and surrendering to Him as Lord. Similarly, Paul concluded his sermon to the Athenians saying:

> Therefore having overlooked the times of ignorance, God is now declaring to men that all everywhere should repent, because He has fixed a day in which He will judge the world in righteousness through a Man whom He has

appointed, having furnished proof to all men by raising Him from the dead (Acts 17:30, 31).

God is 'declaring', 'commandeth' (KJV), 'commands' (NKJV, NIV), not merely requesting, but demanding a response. As the sovereign King He commands and requires 'that all everywhere should repent'.

So our prayer is a prayer that the rule of Christ will come to every heart, that all might be saved, that every knee will bow and every tongue confess the Lordship of Christ (Phil. 2:11). Come Holy Spirit and subdue, conquer and capture all for Your own glory.

God's Rule Now
Second, we are praying that God's rule now will be increasingly acknowledged and obeyed. Reflect again upon the Great Commission:

> And Jesus came up and spoke to them, saying, 'All authority has been given to Me in heaven and on earth. Go therefore and make disciples of all the nations, baptizing them in the name of the Father and the Son and the Holy Spirit, teaching them to observe all that I commanded you; and lo, I am with you always, even to the end of the age' (Matt. 28:18-20).

The point of the commission is not to make mere converts, but disciples. They are to be disciples who are taught to 'observe all that (Christ) commanded (us)'. Christ's kingdom is populated not merely with citizens, but sanctified subjects. Because He is Lord of His realm, His people obey His commands. The goal of the Great Commission and the whole gospel is making disciples.

It is even a vision of nations of disciples. The gospel vision of Isaiah is that of the nations coming to Zion, 'to the mountain of the LORD to the house of the God of Jacob; that He may teach us concerning His ways, and that we may walk in His paths' (Isa. 2:3). They come to our God to be taught. Isaiah continues:

> And many peoples will come and say, 'Come, let us go up to the mountain of the Lord, to the house of the God of Jacob; that He may teach us concerning His ways, and that we may walk in His paths.' For the law will go forth from Zion, and the word of the Lord from Jerusalem. and He will judge between the nations, and will render decisions for many peoples; and they will hammer their swords into plowshares, and their spears into pruning hooks. Nation will not lift up sword against nation, and never again will they learn war (Isa. 2:3, 4).

The law of God is the means by which God extends His rule. 'He will judge between the nations' and His 'law will go forth'. But let us be clear as to how it works. As the gospel changes the hearts of individuals, they go and live their lives in their homes, communities, and the marketplace as Christian citizens. They may submit to Christ sometimes more and sometimes less in their respective spheres. This is true of them personally, and of each realm as a whole. Their family, as a family, may be more or less under the rule of Christ, and more or less pleasing to Him. Their neighborhood, their city, their state, their nation may be more or less under the rule of Christ, and more or less pleasing to Him. The legal system, the educational system, the political system, the social welfare system, the entertainment world, and so on, may be more or less under the rule of Christ and pleasing to Him. My first two years at college I pursued my studies as though being a Christian were one thing and being a student something entirely different, the one having nothing to do with the other. Only later, through reading the writings of the late Francis Schaeffer (e.g. *The God Who is There, How Should We Then Live?*), did I realize that there was a Christian view of psychology, history, literature, art, and even math. All of these can reflect or reject, more or less, a Christian view of God, man, and the world. This is true in every sphere of human endeavor. Our prayer is that in every realm the rule of Christ would be completely and absolutely acknowledged, believed, submitted to, obeyed, and honored. Again, how does this happen? It happens as Christian people with changed hearts begin to recognize inequity, injustice, moral degradation, oppression, vulgarity, violence, inhumanity, and ignorance, and pray that God will change them *and* the cultures to which they belong.

God's Rule Consummated

Third, we are praying that Christ's rule will be completed. We are surrounded, it seems, by inept and corrupt leaders. With the prophets and martyrs we wish to cry out, 'How long, O Lord?' (e.g. Rev. 6:10). How long will we live with foolish and oppressive laws? How long will we live with unjust and confiscatory taxes? How long will we live with immoral and aggrandizing politicians? When will we ever see wise, honest, capable, moral leadership in the nation and in the church? When will we ever see leaders with courage and integrity?

Answer: when the rule of Christ is consummated. So we also cry with the prophets and martyrs, even so, come Lord Jesus! Establish your just and fair and righteous kingdom now!

In the meantime, we work toward that end. The kingdom is not brought about merely by a catastrophic event at the end of time, but incrementally now. Remember the great Nebuchadnezzar, walking on his roof in Babylon, surveying the great city and saying:

> 'Is this not Babylon the great, which I myself have built as a royal residence by the might of my power and for the glory of my majesty?' (Dan. 4:30).

God determined to make an example of Nebuchadnezzar:

> While the word was in the king's mouth, a voice came from heaven, saying, 'King Nebuchadnezzar, to you it is declared: sovereignty has been removed from you, and you will be driven away from mankind, and your dwelling place will be with the beasts of the field. You will be given grass to eat like cattle, and seven periods of time will pass over you, until you recognize that the Most High is ruler over the realm of mankind, and bestows it on whomever He wishes' (Dan. 4:31, 32).

What did God demand? That Nebuchadnezzar 'recognize that the Most High is ruler over the realm of mankind'. For seven years Nebuchadnezzar lived like a madman. No, it was worse than that. He lived like an animal. He 'began eating grass like cattle', his hair grew 'like eagles feathers and his nails like bird claws' (Dan. 4:33). Only when he humbled himself, and 'raised (his) eyes toward heaven', did his reason return, and he confess God's sovereign rule:

> '... and I blessed the Most High and praised and honored Him who lives forever; for His dominion is an everlasting dominion, and His kingdom endures from generation to generation. And all the inhabitants of the earth are accounted as nothing, but He does according to His will in the host of heaven and among the inhabitants of earth; and no one can ward off His hand or say to Him, "What hast Thou done?"' (Dan. 4:34b-35)

The submission of Nebuchadnezzar to the 'Most High' is a paradigm of the future. One day all worldly powers will submit. If even the wicked, pagan king of Babylon could be brought to his knees, and similarly if even mighty Rome could be humbled, who can resist His will? We pray that God's kingdom will 'crush and put an end to all (the) kingdoms' of the world and will itself 'endure forever' (Dan. 2:44; cf Dan. 7:13, 14); that like the mustard seed, it will grow to highest prominence in the garden (Matt. 13:31, 32); that like yeast it will leaven the whole loaf (Matt. 13:33). We are praying that the kingdom will be established 'on earth, as it is in heaven', that the kingdoms of this world will become the kingdom of our Lord and His Christ (Rev. 11:15).

Why do we pray these things? Why do we pray for them even before we ask for bread? Because by praying we are 'looking for and hastening the coming of the day of God' (2 Pet. 3:12). Somehow our prayers help us bring about that thing for which we pray, even the consummation of Christ's kingdom at the *end*, and its incremental growth *now*. We long to see the rule of Christ established. We cannot bear to see the authority of Christ ignored. When the word of Christ is not believed and not obeyed, and unbelievers scoff at and ridicule the faith and the faithful, we *long* to see the great reversal, when every blaspheming mouth is closed and Christ and His kingdom is manifest even to the skeptics; when every stronghold and every lofty thing raised up against the knowledge of God is torn down, and every thought is taken captive to the obedience of Christ (2 Cor. 10:4, 5); when every knee bows and every tongue confesses that Jesus is Lord (Phil. 2:11). For all this we pray when we pray 'Thy kingdom come ... on earth, as it is in heaven'. The *Shorter Catechism* summarizes:

Q. *What do we pray for in the second petition?*
A. In the second petition, (which is, *Thy kingdom come,*) we pray, that Satan's kingdom may be destroyed; and that the kingdom of grace may be advanced, ourselves and others brought into it, and kept in it; and that the kingdom of glory may be hastened.

8

Thy Will Be Done

The third of the three parallel opening petitions of the Lord's Prayer is, 'Thy will be done, on earth as it is in heaven'. The name of God is to be hallowed, as we have seen, by His kingdom coming and His will being done. We have looked at the former, and now we shall examine the latter.

There is considerable confusion about what is meant by the 'will' of God and what we are to make of it. As unbelievable as it seems to me today, I was actually taught during my college years by very earnest and devout Christian people not to pray 'Thy will be done'. 'Tell God what *you* want', they urged me. 'If you conclude your prayer with 'if it be your will' or something of this sort you'll cancel out your request', they said. 'God will do what *He* planned rather than what *you* want'. I trust that it is obvious that this formulation of things will not do. After all, there is no mistaking that Jesus *is* teaching us to pray, 'Thy will be done'! There is also no mistaking that God doing *His* will is to be preferred to His doing *our* will. In fact, Packer says, 'Here more clearly than anywhere the purpose of prayer becomes plain: not to make God do my will (which is practicing magic), but to bring my will into line with His' (151).

What is meant by God's 'will'? There are two clear meanings in Scripture which sometimes seem to be in conflict with each other.

God's Will Defined
First, 'God's will' sometimes designates God's preceptive will. Used in this sense it indicates what God commands (i.e. His precepts), requires, or desires of us. Jesus says, 'he who does the will of My Father who is in heaven' will enter the kingdom of heaven. 'Will' here is what God has commanded (Matt. 7:21). See also here:

> For whoever does the will of My Father who is in heaven, he is My brother and sister and mother (Matt. 12:50).

'Will' could only mean God's revealed will, His precepts.

The Psalmist says,

> I delight to do Thy will, O my God; Thy Law is within my heart (Ps. 40:8).

'Will' and 'law' parallel one another. They are equivalents. The Apostle Paul says,

> For this is the will of God, your sanctification (1 Thess. 4:3).

'Will' here is what He has commanded, what He wants, what He wishes, and what He desires. Similarly the Apostle Paul says that God:

> desires all men to be saved and to come to the knowledge of the truth (1 Tim. 2:4).

What is translated 'desires' is the same word translated elsewhere 'will' (*thel_ma*). In all the above cases 'will' or 'desire' indicates not God's sovereign will, or what He has decreed. Some will be lost. The salvation of 'all men' is what God commands, wants, desires, wishes. Jesus says of the one lost sheep out of a hundred:

> Thus it is not the will of your Father who is in heaven that one of these little ones perish (Matt. 18:14).

This too is what God commands (i.e. that all be found, that all repent, that all believe), what He wills, wishes, wants, desires. But little ones do perish.

Second, 'God's will' sometimes designates God's decretive or sovereign will. By this we mean that which God decrees, plans and determines shall actually happen and cannot but happen. Thus in the Garden of Gethsemane Jesus prays one way but acknowledges another 'will' which the Father may have planned:

> And He went a little beyond them, and fell on His face and prayed, saying, 'My Father, if it is possible, let this cup pass from Me; yet not as I will, but as Thou wilt' (Matt. 26:39).

It was certainly not the 'will' of God in a *preceptive* sense that wicked men should crucify the Lord of glory. In fact, it violated God's explicit will regarding justice. How then was the crucifixion God's will? In the *decretive* sense.

Paul wishes to come to the Romans but realizes that God may not *will* it or *plan* it.

> For God, whom I serve in my spirit in the preaching of the gospel of His Son, is my witness

as to how unceasingly I make mention of you, always in my prayers making request, if perhaps now at last by the will of God I may succeed in coming to you (Rom. 1:9, 10).

I will come, He says, only if God sovereignly wills. Similarly, the people of Caesarea beg Paul not to go to Jerusalem where he'll encounter trouble. But when he insists on going they conclude:

'The will of the Lord be done!' (Acts 21:14).

This 'will' is the sovereign plan of God. The plan of God shall stand, they are saying.

James teaches us not to make plans for the future, saying 'I will go here and do thus and so', as if we had the power to execute them.

Instead, you ought to say, 'if the Lord wills, we shall live and also do this or that' (Jas. 4:15).

We may perhaps use Nebuchadnezzar's prayer as a summary of what the will of God means in this second sense:

But He does according to His will in the host of heaven and among the inhabitants of earth; and no one can ward off His hand or say to Him, 'What hast Thou done?' (Dan. 4:35).

God does 'according to His will' in heaven and on earth. He executes His sovereign plan. This is what we call 'providence'. He 'works all things after the counsel of His will' (Eph. 1:11), decreeing (in the language of the

Westminster Confession of Faith) 'whatsoever comes to pass'. In this sense the 'will' of God is what God has decreed, predestined, planned, ordained or permitted actually to take place. The will of God in this sense includes everything that ever happens, from the creation to the fall, to the cross, to the consummation.

The will of God then is either what God *commands* or what God sovereignly *ordains*. Sometimes a given event is God's will in both senses, as when the apostles obey the Great Commission (Matt. 28:18) and preach. When they actually preach at a given time and place they are doing what God commands and has decreed should happen. But sometimes what God commands and what He decrees seem to contradict each other. The cross is the supreme example of this. In Acts we read,

> 'For truly in this city there were gathered together against Thy holy servant Jesus, whom Thou didst anoint, both Herod and Pontius Pilate, along with the Gentiles and the peoples of Israel, to do whatever Thy hand and Thy purpose predestined to occur' (Acts 4:27, 28; cf Acts 2:23).

At the cross, what God commands (that we do not murder, that we do justice, that we honor His Son, etc.) came into direct conflict with what He 'predestined to occur' (that a Savior should be provided for His elect, that He should be judicially murdered, that He should be humiliated, mocked, blasphemed, etc.).

Ultimately this apparent contradiction (we say apparent because all is harmony in the mind of God and we are skeptical about our ability to perceive the divine consistency this side of eternity) is reconciled at the consummation. Then the 'last enemy' will be defeated and all things will be in subjection to Christ (1 Cor. 15:24-28). Then what God desires will be fully accomplished and what He commands will be coextensive with what He decrees. The decretive and preceptive wills shall be one.

There is yet another sense in which the will of God is sometimes spoken about. *This we might call God's 'secret' will.* This is not what God has commanded (which isn't a secret) or what God decreed (which is a secret, but He's not telling – Deut. 29:29), but what He *really* wants us to do or what He really wants to happen in a given circumstance. For example, when choosing between job A or job B, both of which are God-pleasing alternatives, people will often ask what the will of God is. What do they mean? They aren't asking what has God *commanded*. Then the decision would be easy, say if the choice were between taking a job with the General Motors or with organized crime. They aren't asking what God has *decreed* because, as we've noted, God isn't telling, and besides that's going to happen anyway. They want to know what God *really* wants them to do. Let me gently say that the will of God in this sense doesn't exist. There is no *third* will of God. This area outside of what He has commanded is known as the realm of Christian liberty. What God 'wants' is for us to obey His revealed will, make wise decisions and do what we want. This idea that we have to somehow divine what God wants beyond what He tells us through His word can be oppressive and paralyzing. It destroys Christian liberty. Many people are crippled in the decision-making process because they are searching for this hidden will of God. Shall I marry person A, person B, or remain single? They torture themselves trying to find out what God wants but hasn't revealed. What the Bible says, however, is if the persons otherwise are approved by God, do what you want. The Apostle Paul says to the single, if you want to marry, marry. If not, remain single. 'Let him do what he wishes' (1 Cor. 7:20-40)!

Praying for God's Will to Be Done

When we pray 'Thy will be done', we are asking both that God will be obeyed and that He will bring history to the glorious conclusion which He has ordained. We pray for 'both moral obedience and the bringing to pass of certain events', says Carson (170). What events? Events such as the defeat of evil, the conversion of the nations, the conversion of the Jews, the rule of righteousness, and the return of Christ. We pray that God's will, as commanded and as decreed, will be fully accomplished on earth to the same extent (completely) and in the same way (freely, openly, spontaneously) as it is in heaven.

First, we are praying that the preceptive will of God be obeyed. We are identifying ourselves totally with the will of God as commanded in His word. Our passion and prayer is that God's will be done in our lives and throughout the whole world. Consequently, we are zealous for the word of God. 'O how I love Thy law', we cry with the Psalmist (Ps. 119:97). We treasure it in our hearts (Ps. 119:11). It is more desirable to us than gold, and sweeter to us than honey (Ps. 19:10). We find that in keeping it there is great reward (Ps. 19:11). We find the commandments not to be 'burdensome', but a blessing (1 John 5:3). We pray this because we can hope for nothing more – O that I should fulfill the will of God! That I should love as I ought, serve as I ought, be holy as I ought, and bear fruit for Your kingdom as I ought! Let me do your will in my marriage, with my family, in the church, in the workplace, in the community, in the nation! And we are praying that everyone else would do the same! 'We pray that God's laws may be obeyed by men as perfectly, readily, and unceasingly as they are by angels in heaven' says J. C. Ryle (52).

Second, we are praying that God's decretive will be accepted. This is perhaps the more difficult of the two senses in which to pray this prayer. 'Thy will be done', is not only an aspiration and hope, but an act of submission.

> When peace, like a river, attendeth my way,
> When sorrows like sea billows roll;
> Whatever my lot, thou has taught me to say,
> 'It is well, it is well with my soul.'

When tragedy strikes, are you able to accept the will of God? Are you able to say, 'It is well with my soul'? I have found that at times it is not just the tragic event, but the timing of it that seems so difficult to accept. Emily's father died just a month before the birth of the first grandchild. That was hard for the family to handle. They wrestled with not only the tragedy of his death (at fifty-four) but that he would never know his first grandchild. I know a couple who planned all their married life for retirement, accumulated a hefty nest egg and, just as he retired, suddenly and unexpectedly he died. His widow had an awful time dealing with that. Well-meaning people try to absolve God of responsibility for these things, seeking to explain why bad things happen to good people. They say such things are *not* the will of God during tragedy. God didn't want that to happen, they'll say. But instinctively people know better. That's why even pagans shake their fists at God. Everyone knows that ultimately God ordains, or at least permits, *or at least determines not to prevent* a sad event. 'The Lord gives and the Lord takes away'(Job 1:21). Why does He do this? Because it is His will. Because it suits His good purposes. Because it fits His plan. Because God is infinite and we are finite, because God is holy and we are corrupt, because God is omniscient and we are foolish and ignorant. And because God is good and we are evil, we trust that He knows what He is doing. Consequently we pray, 'Thy will be done'. We submit to His will. We trust His plan. The praying of this petition 'takes some praying', as Packer notes (153). It requires meekness and humility, faith and trust. How else could one sing these words?

> Whate'er my God ordains is right:
> His holy will abideth;
> I will be still whate'er he doth,
> And follow where He guideth.
> He is my God;
> Though dark my road,
> He holds me that I shall not fall:
> Wherefore to Him I leave it all.

It is never easy to affirm 'whate'er my God ordains is right', or 'wherefore to Him I leave it all'. It is never easy to say, 'you meant it for evil but God meant it for good' (Gen. 50:20). We are praying for the grace so to see and so to speak when we pray this petition.

Third, we are praying for the will of God (preceptive and decretive) to be fully accomplished. We pray that God will hasten (2 Pet. 3:12) the day when His will will be done on earth as it is in heaven. Thus we anticipate in this petition the day when history will come to the glorious consummation that God has willed for it, that consummation for which all creation groans, as it awaits 'the freedom of the glory of the children of God' (Rom. 8:21). Then the will of God will be realized all the time. There will be no more sin, no more evil, no more devil, no more sorrow, no more pain, no more tears (Rev. 21:1-6). For this we long. For this we pray. 'Thy will be done, on earth, even as it is in heaven'. The *Shorter Catechism* summarizes in this way:

Q. *What do we pray for in the third petition?*
A. In the third petition, which is, *Thy will be done in earth, as it is in heaven,* we pray that God, by his grace, would make us able and willing to know, obey, and submit to his will in all things, as the angels do in heaven.

'To know, obey, and submit to His will in all things, as the angels do in heaven', is our prayer.

9

Our Daily Bread

On one of his many visits to Great Britain, D L Moody asked an assembly of children in Edinburgh the question, 'what is prayer?', expecting no answer and anticipating answering the question himself. To his amazement, dozens of little hands shot up. Calling upon one at random, the young boy answered:

> Prayer is an offering up of our desires unto God for things agreeable to his will, in the name of Christ, with confession of our sins, and thankful acknowledgment of his mercies (*Shorter Catechism*, question #98).

A delighted Mr. Moody responded, 'thank God, my boy, that you were born in Scotland'.[1]

Order
The beautiful answer of the *Shorter Catechism* that the children of Scotland once committed to memory highlights the harmony that is to exist between our desires and the will of God. We offer 'our desires' in

---

[1] *The Kneeling Christian*, 53

prayer, a great privilege for sure, but for things 'agreeable to his will' and in a spirit of confession and thanksgiving.

As we turn to what Douglas Kelly calls the 'manward' side of the Lord's Prayer, we do not now transgress the whole mood and tone established by the 'preface' and the 'godward' petitions.

The order of the Lord's Prayer should continue to influence us as our personal petitions are offered. As we turn from God's glory to our needs we are to do so without losing sight of the ultimate ends for which we are praying. As we pray for bread, we are still to seek first the kingdom of God. 'So whenever we pray', says Calvin, 'we must not drop our eyes from the target' (209). 'Temporal things must be prayed for for spiritual ends', says Thomas Watson. And again, 'We must aim at heaven while we are praying for earth' (199). The God-centered frame of reference established by the preface and first three petitions is not now dropped. Rather we continue to pray in the same manner even as we pray for personal things. When we pray for the necessities of life (which we take 'bread' to represent) we do so with the aim that 'whether (we) eat or drink or whatever (we) do' we do it 'all to the glory of God' (1 Cor. 10:31). Simply, 'those who truly pray the first three petitions thereby commit themselves to live wholly for God', says Packer, 'and the natural and logical next request is for food to give them energy for this' (158). In other words, I should not now begin to pray from a temporal, worldly or secular point of view. Can this be a problem? James said it was:

> You ask and do not receive, because you ask with wrong motives, so that you may spend it on your pleasures (Jas. 4:3).

One may pray with 'wrong motives'. To have no higher ends in view than wealth to 'spend' on one's 'pleasures' is sinful and wrong. Thomas Watson comments:

> One man is sick, and he prays for health that he may be among his cups and harlots; another prays for an estate; he would not only have his belly filled, but his barns; and he would be rich that he may raise his name, or that, having more power in his hand, he may now take a fuller revenge on his enemies. It is impiety joined with impudence to pray to God to give us temporal things that we may be the better enabled to serve the devil (199).

As I begin now to pray for the necessities of life, I must do so as one who is still seeking the glory of God's name, kingdom, and will. It must never become a self-centered exercise pursued for selfish ends. I seek temporal things in prayer, not so that I will be 'better enabled to serve the devil', but better enabled to serve God.

Meaning

What then are we seeking when we pray, 'Give us this day our daily bread'?

First, we are seeking from the hand of God all the necessities of life. 'Bread' sometimes represents just bread, as in a loaf of bread, and sometimes signifies all forms of food (Gen. 3:19; Prov. 30:8; Mark 3:20; Acts 6:1; 2 Thess. 3:12; Jas. 2:15). Luther and others have argued that by extension it indicates all we need in the physical realm: 'food, a healthy body, good weather, house, home, wife, children, good government, and peace' (quoted in Stott, 149). 'Man does not live by *bread* alone' is a good example of this broader meaning. Jesus there uses 'bread' to represent all of material life (Matt. 4:4). Dickson defines it here as 'whatsoever we make use of for our subsistence' (73). Murray's conclusion: 'the whole earthly life is given over to the Father's loving care' (34).

Consequently, when we pray this petition we are acknowledging our entire dependence upon God for at least all our *physical* needs. From where do we get our food, clothing, shelter, health, and wealth? From the hand of God. Since this is so, there is no shame in seeking material things from Him. One is not 'unspiritual' for seeking health and material provision in prayer. Neither is it 'low-grade prayer' as some consider it (Packer, 158). The Apostle John prays for his readers:

> 'Beloved, I pray that in all respects you may prosper and be in good health, just as your soul prospers' (3 John 2).

Go ahead and pray for prosperity and health. Consider the opposite. Failure to offer such a prayer for physical necessities may imply belief in one's self-sufficiency. Our neglect of the material realm in prayer would argue that we think that we are able to take care of ourselves, and supply all our needs; that we don't seek God's help because we don't need it. Or it might imply that we don't pray because we are convinced that God doesn't care about these things. Bread and such things are too mundane, too unimportant, too carnal for God's concern. But when we pray, 'Give us this day our daily bread', we are acknowledging that, a) God cares about our material needs; b) it is appropriate to pray that our material needs will be met; and c) the only source for all our physical necessities is the hand of God. We are looking to God and to no one else, not even ourselves, to meet our material needs. When we pray this petition we are confessing that all that we are, and all that we ever will be, is ours only through His mercy and grace. The Apostle Paul put it this way to the proud Corinthians and likewise to us today:

> For who regards you as superior? And what do you have that you did not receive? But if you did receive it, why do you boast as if you had not received it? (1 Cor. 4:7).

'What do you have that you did not receive?' he asks. Isn't it true that you owe it all to God? If you have it, God gave it. God said to his people Israel through Moses:

> But you shall remember the Lord your God, for it is He who is giving you power to make wealth, that He may confirm His covenant which He swore to your fathers, as it is this day (Deut. 8:18).

Do you have wealth? Then God gave you the ability or 'power' to make it. He has ordered all the variables that make it possible: health, family stability, education, providential opportunities, wisdom, and knowledge are all His gifts. Rearrange a few of them and the 'power' to make wealth disappears. 'Every good thing bestowed and every perfect gift is from above, coming down from the Father of lights' (Jas. 1:17).

All of this implies both humility and gratitude, doesn't it? This is why the Apostle Paul asks, 'why do you boast as if you had not received it?' I am not a 'self-made' man. God made me. I cannot boast about any particular faculty, aptitude, or opportunity that I might have. So what if I am smart or beautiful or powerful or wealthy? The same God has made us all and distributes His gifts as He desires (1 Cor. 12:7, 11, 18). 'Why do you boast as if you had not received it?'

Since this is so, gratitude ought to flood our souls. Look at the abundance that we enjoy from our good and gracious God. We pray for bread because it is His gift to us *along with everything else*. If I am to eat, He must give. If I am to drink, to have shelter, to have clothing, to have a job, to get an education, have a family, have children, and so on, He must give them. Convinced of this, I pour out my soul in prayer pleading for those things which are necessary.

Can we extend the bread metaphor further into *spiritual* realms also? Can the necessities that we seek from God's hand under the rubric of 'bread' include spiritual bread?

Consider this: Why is it that Jesus instructs us to pray for bread before we pray for the forgiveness of our sins? Isn't the soul more important than the body? Have you never pondered this matter? Don't be alarmed. Of the thirteen different commentators that I consulted, only Calvin and Lloyd-Jones thought to raise the issue. The latter thinks Jesus prays for bread first because physical existence must be maintained before spiritual concerns can be addressed. If we die we can no longer prayerfully give attention to our souls. But this answer does not explain why the preface and Godward petitions would have preceded the petition for bread. If maintaining our physical existence is such a priority, why would the petition for bread not be the first thing out of our mouths? Calvin, on the other hand, suggests that 'bread' is a comprehensive word indicating all our necessities, spiritual and temporal. He argues that this is an example of condescension of Christ's part 'in order to lead us higher from such elementary things'. He continues,

> So we do not ask to be given our daily bread before we are reconciled to God, as though the passing diet of the stomach were worth more than the salvation of our eternal soul, but our thoughts ascend from earth to heaven, as by the rungs of a ladder. When God condescends to feed our bodies, certainly it is over our spiritual life that He is most concerned. Thus His kindly favour swells our confidence (209).

Bread comes first because bread represents *all* our needs, spiritual and physical. 'All innocent and legitimate desires can also be requested in this part of the prayer', says Blaiklock (37). Certainly the *immediate* point of application is physical bread. We don't want to minimize this. We don't want to make the mistake of many in the early church who completely spiritualized bread because it was viewed as being worldly to care about physical needs. It is right and proper to care about physical needs. God cares about our physical needs. God cares about our bodies. Jesus healed and fed bodies during his earthly ministry. The 'word became flesh' (John 1:14). But even as physical bread it stands alone among these personal petitions as addressing material concerns. 'Note the proportion', Pink urges. 'This teaches us that in prayer as in all other activities of life, temporal concerns are to be subordinated to spiritual concerns' (106,107).

Let us then climb the 'rungs' of Calvin's 'ladder' and understand the spiritual significance of bread. 'Bread' is often used metaphorically to indicate spiritual food. Jesus Himself is the 'bread of life' (John 6:35). Jesus said:

'I am the living bread that came down out of heaven; if anyone eats of this bread, he shall live forever; and the bread also which I shall give for the life of the world is My flesh' (John 6:51).

Again He said:

'For My flesh is true food, and My blood is true drink' (John 6:55).

Given this important spiritual metaphor, the petition for 'bread' may rightly be understood as prayer for all our spiritual necessities. We are acknowledging that from God alone can we expect to receive all that is necessary for our spiritual life. How are we convicted of our sin? By the Holy Spirit (John 16:8). How are we born again? By the Holy Spirit (John 3:1ff). How are we sanctified? By the Spirit of Christ (1 Cor. 1:30). How do we become Christ-like? How do we come to enjoy the fruits of love, joy, peace, and self-control? By the Spirit of God (Gal. 5:22, 23). How do we bear fruit for God's kingdom? Only by abiding in Christ (John 15:1ff).

Spiritual self-sufficiency may be more of a problem than we realize. Our personal prayerlessness and our congregational prayerlessness may be symptoms of this. We tend to have a high level of confidence in our ability to solve problems and make things happen. So we turn to new programs, new methods, new strategies. We multiply meetings and studies. We conduct surveys and polls. We bounce from conference to conference. Do we really believe that though we plant and water that God must cause the growth (1 Cor. 3:6)? That Christ must build His church (Matt. 16:18)? That God must give the increase (e.g. Acts 5:14; 6:7)?

There is nothing spiritually good for which we could ever claim credit. We owe it all to Christ. Left to ourselves we are dead in our trespasses and sins (Eph. 2:1ff), dead to the things of God, blind to the glory of God, deaf to the voice of God, lost in darkness that we love, marching down the broad path that leads to destruction (John 3:19-21; Matt. 7:13, 14). Knowing this we turn to God in prayer and seek our spiritual bread from Him. From Him alone we receive the power to believe, obey, grow, and persevere. If he were to loosen His grip upon us we would fail and fall. So we pray, 'give us this day our *spiritual* bread'. We are utterly dependent upon Christ for all spiritual nourishment, progress, and growth.

Second, we are seeking from the hand of God these necessities of life on a daily basis. Not only are we to depend upon God for everything, but we are to do so *every day*. 'Give us this day' implies a daily prayer. The word translated 'daily' (*epiousios*) is found only in the Lord's Prayer and nowhere else in the New Testament, or in all of the Greek literature outside of the New Testament. Its meaning has perplexed commentators going all the way back to Origen. The suggested options range from 'daily' to 'the coming day's' to 'necessary'. Most commentators believe it means the first or second of these options. Regardless, we are being taught to pray daily ('give us *this* day') for the food we need (whether 'daily bread', the 'coming day's bread', or for the 'necessary bread' of that day). If it were prayed in the morning, it would be a prayer for the food of that day; if in the evening, for the coming day. Consequently, Jesus is deliberately cultivating a way of relating to God. How so?

Application

First, Jesus is teaching us to pray daily. He might have taught us to pray weekly or monthly or yearly. He might have taught an annual prayer, 'Give us this *year* the food of the coming year'. Then we'd be done with prayer for 365 days. Or, He might have taught a weekly prayer, 'Give us this *week* the food of the coming week'. But instead, He teaches daily prayer expressing daily dependence upon God. This is a distinctive way of relating to God that differs from that which would have resulted from weekly, monthly, or yearly prayers. Every day we go to Him to ask for that which only He can give. A daily relationship, a daily walk (at least) is being encouraged. For years I have wondered if the Bible really teaches what I have been taught and taught others to practice – a daily devotional. Well, here it is, staring us in the face – 'Give us this day'. Here also is daily corporate worship – 'Give *us*', He says. This is a daily group prayer. The standard Protestant practice since the time of the Reformation has been to conduct weekday prayer in the home and Lord's Day prayer in the church. But whether it's family prayer or congregational prayer, Jesus clearly envisions daily prayer gatherings by His disciples. Why? Dependence upon God is our actual state of existence, and so it is to be expressed daily.

Probably I have made the statement to every Inquirers' Class (what our church calls its new members' class) we've had over the last thirteen years, that one spiritual meal a week will never do. Daily we turn to Him not only for 'bread alone' but for 'every word that proceeds from the mouth of God' (Matt. 4:4). Daily we should pray. Daily we should meditate upon God's word. We should 'pray without ceasing', that is, without interrupting our daily prayer disciplines (1 Thess. 5:17). Why? Is this a new legalism? Are we being ordered to conform to a rigid prayer calendar? No, we are being taught to pray daily, because we are weak and needy. Jesus is expecting daily prayer because we are to depend moment by moment upon the sustaining power of God. Only as we abide in Him can we do anything (John 15:4, 5). Jesus is teaching absolute dependence on our heavenly Father, both for our physical and spiritual sustenance. Daily we are to pray. Daily we are to pray for bread.

But what if our shelves are stocked and our barns are full? Then it is hard to see in what sense we could be said to depend upon God. After all, I only have to open the refrigerator if I need food, right? No, in a significant sense, this is wrong. It is wrong simply because the power of that food to nourish comes directly, moment by moment, from God. Calvin recognizes the potential for misunderstanding among those who have an abundance.

Now, the objection is raised, that since it is certain that Christ set this common rule of prayer before all godly people, and yet that there are some rich men in that number who have a capital sum saved up, how can He be telling them to ask for what they already have in their own homes, and to seek for one day what would do them very well for a year. The solution is simple. These words tell us that unless God feeds us, no amount of accrued capital will mean anything. Although grain, wine, and everything else be there to overflowing, if they do not have the dew of God's unseen benediction, these all vanish on the spot, or their enjoyment is taken away, or the power they have to nourish us is lost, and we starve in the midst of our great supply. So there is no wonder that Christ invites the rich and poor alike to the heavenly store (210).

Every day God must bless or our food will do us no good. Consequently, because we eat daily, we should pray daily. The principle being taught is that of continual dependence upon God. Daily prayer means recognition of continual dependence upon God for our sustenance.

Second, Jesus is teaching us to live one day at a time. Jesus will expand on this principle at much greater length later in Matthew 6 (vv. 25-34). This petition anticipates that teaching. We are not to request or expect more than a day's provision because we are to live one day at a time. Remember this was written during an era when most workers received only a day's wage at a time. They were always within a day or two of disaster. If, because of illness or some other reason, they could not work, they would not eat nor would their families. Thus Jesus instructs us to ask God for only one day's provision of bread at a time, and to trust Him for the next. This does not mean that we don't *plan* for the future. Neither does it mean that we don't *work* to accumulate a supply. Prayer is not a replacement for planning or labor. But it does mean that we don't *worry* about the future. Jesus goes on to tell His disciples:

> Therefore do not be anxious for tomorrow; for tomorrow will care for itself. Each day has enough trouble of its own (Matt. 6:34).

Day-by-day reliance upon God is being taught by the Lord in His prayer. Jesus does not encourage us to seek a month's supply so that we might then go on 'in forgetfulness of God', as Morris puts it (147). He wants us to be continually conscious of our dependence, and so teaches a *daily* dependence, a dependence about which we are reminded daily, a dependence that is expressed daily in prayer.

Devotional guides entitled, 'The Daily Walk', or 'Our Daily Bread', or 'Morning & Evening' were written with this insight in mind. We are to keep close tabs, close accounts with God. We need sustenance from Him every day if we are to live. We are to seek from Him that sustenance not in year-long, month-long, or even week-long chunks, but every day. Each day we are to live for that day.

Why is this important? Because we all tend to live like atheists. When our barns are full we forget about God and behave as though we don't need Him. God warned Israel to beware,

> ... lest, when you have eaten and are satisfied, and have built good houses and lived in them, and when your herds and your flocks multiply, and your

silver and gold multiply, and all that you have multiplies, then your heart becomes proud, and you forget the Lord your God who brought you out from the land of Egypt, out of the house of slavery (Deut. 8:12-14).

Full barns lead to forgetful hearts. This is why the Proverbs say:

Give me neither poverty nor riches; feed me with the food that is my portion, lest I be full and deny Thee and say, "Who is the Lord?" Or lest I be in want and steal, and profane the name of my God (Prov. 30:8, 9).

Those are two temptations against which this petition is directed. One is to have little and cease trusting in God's provision and steal. The other is to become full 'and deny Thee'. Daily provision means daily dependence, renewed with the advent of each new day.

For us to pray this way we must live contentedly with what we have (Phil. 4:11, 12). No, our barns may not be full. Our Father may answer our prayer and supply no more than a single day's blessing. We may not have supplies for months or years to come. But the consequence will be that we will live in close dependence upon God.

Here, then, is how we might pray this petition. As we begin to consider that God supplies us with our daily bread our hearts would be filled with thanksgiving. With grateful hearts we would forget none of His benefits (Ps. 103:1, 2).

'O Lord', we would pray, 'we give thanks in everything (1 Thess. 5:18). We recognize that You have given every good and perfect gift (Jas. 1:17). There is nothing that we have that we haven't received (1 Cor. 4:7). It has not been by our might or power that we enjoy an abundance, but by Your blessing (Dan. 4:30). And so we seek from You all that we need for life and godliness (2 Pet. 1:3).'

We might then focus on our material needs.

'We pray for food and drink with which to nourish, sustain, and refresh our bodies; for homes to provide safe shelter from the elements and evildoers; for clothing with which to cover our fleshly tabernacle; for protection from all manner of injury or harm; for good health, strength, and mobility. Provide us, we pray, with all that we need for our physical well-being.'

Then we might begin to pray for our spiritual well-being.

'We pray also for our souls. Bless the church and its ministry to us. Feed us the bread of life through the ministry of the word and sacraments. Anoint our ministers and teachers as they administer the means of grace. Provide us with the fellowship we need to grow in Christ. Use Your word as it is read, sung, taught, and prayed in public worship and in our family devotions. Grant us the power and presence of your Holy Spirit. Conform us more and more to the image of God (Eph. 5:1ff). Bear the fruit of the Spirit in us (Gal. 5:19ff). Enable us this day to walk by the Spirit. Enable us this day to abide in Christ, knowing that apart from Him we can do nothing' (John 15:5).

The piety behind the Lord's Prayer is both *God-centered* and *God-dependent*. We are to live and pray for the glory of God, and live and pray in conscious dependence upon God, repudiating all claims of self-sufficiency, forsaking all pretensions of self-reliance, and praying daily for our daily sustenance, both physical and spiritual.

10

Forgive Us Our Debts

The second of the 'manward' petitions, and fifth overall, is this:

Forgive us our debts, as we forgive our debtors

'As bread is the first need of the body', says Andrew Murray, 'so forgiveness is for the soul' (34). If we have overly spiritualized part of our understanding of the fourth petition (for daily bread), this petition, combined with the next, gives to the prayer a clear spiritual priority over our physical needs. Food is sought for the body, but both forgiveness and protection from temptation and evil are sought in this and the next petition. What do our souls need? They need deliverance from the *penalty* and *power* of sin. 'Forgive us our debts' and 'lead us not into temptation'. This is the crucial thing. How often when we pray (which I hope we do often) do we pray only for our bodies and material well-being? How often in prayer meetings and on prayer lists do the overwhelming number of prayer items listed, discussed, and prayed for have to do with health and physical matters? This is not the priority of the Lord's Prayer. Jesus prays first and foremost for the glory, the name, the kingdom, and the will of God. When He does turn to personal petitions, they are 'spiritual' requests – for the essentials of life ('bread'), and for forgiveness and holiness. Jesus' priorities are the Biblical priorities. One can see them, for example, in Paul's prayers for his churches, as in Philippians 1, Ephesians 1, and Colossians 1. He says nothing about their health, their vocations, or their finances. He prays instead for their souls. So it is here. Because our main concern is with God's glory and honor we begin with praise, move on to petitions for His greater praise, and then finally offer petitions concerned mainly for our ability to live for His praise. What is Jesus teaching us in this petition?

Pray for Forgiveness

First, Jesus is teaching us to pray daily for the forgiveness of our sins. This is a believer's prayer. It begins 'Our Father'. It is a daily prayer. Its frame of reference is 'this day'. Consequently, we learn that daily prayers of confession are an important part of the Christian prayer. Christians sin. They have 'debts'. Confession is the right response to their sins. This is a point that needs to be made in light of some unfortunate teaching that says the opposite. Some have argued that at the time of our initial repentance and faith in Christ, all of our sins – past, present and future – are forgiven. This being the case, they say, we need not continue to ask for forgiveness, since we have has already received it once and for all. Some would go so far as to see post-conversion confession as a positively harmful thing. It shows a lack of faith, they'd say. Don't you believe the gospel? Don't you believe that the blood of Christ cleanses us from *all* sin? Your confession of sin reveals unbelief, they insist.

How are we to answer this? We would urge the following:

1. *Recognize the priority of Scripture over logic.* Somewhere their line of reasoning has gone off track, because Jesus clearly teaches here the necessity of ongoing confession of sin, of daily confession as part of this daily prayer. When this happens (and periodically it does) one must beat a hasty retreat to Scripture, reaffirming its clear instruction over our theological reasoning.

2. *Recognize the difference between the 'already' and the 'not yet'.* In one sense we are forgiven (Col. 1:14), sanctified (1 Cor. 1:30), seated with Christ (Eph. 2:6), and glorified (Rom. 8:30). Yet this 'already' aspect of our position in Christ in no way invalidates the need for all the means involved in the process of getting there, such as ongoing faith, obedience, holiness, prayer, and perseverence. Though our glorification is so certain that the past tense (the Greek aorist) can be used, yet the process is necessary. We *are* saved and we *shall be* saved. To deny this is to plunge into fatalism. Have we been blessed in Christ with 'every spiritual blessing' (Eph. 1:3)? Have we been made complete in Him (Col. 2:10)? Has God granted us 'everything pertaining to life and godliness through the knowledge of Him' (2 Pet. 1:3)? The answers, of course, are yes, yes, yes. Then do we still need to receive those blessings? After all, aren't we already 'complete'? Don't we already have 'everything'? Then why do we need to continue to seek His grace? Because we have them already in *principle* and in *part*, but not in their *fullness* and *completion*. Our receiving of 'every spiritual blessing' is certain but not yet fully realized. In the meantime, we will have

to continue to seek Christ's grace and blessing through the Word, sacraments, prayer, and the fellowship of the saints.

With respect to the forgiveness of sin, we obtain it for the sins of today through confession. At the time of our conversion all of our past sins were forgiven. Subsequent to that time, we continue to receive forgiveness only as we confess our sins. Is this not why we are told to confess our sins? Is this not why we need an advocate? How are we to make sense of the teaching of 1 John if this is not so?

> If we say that we have no sin, we are deceiving ourselves, and the truth is not in us. If we confess our sins, He is faithful and righteous to forgive us our sins and to cleanse us from all unrighteousness (1 John 1:8, 9).

The statements are conditional. *If* we confess our sins we are forgiven and cleansed. Conversely it must be that if we do not confess our sins, if we do not acknowledge that we sin, there is no forgiveness for us. Forgiveness, like grace, must be continually received.

> My little children, I am writing these things to you that you may not sin. And if anyone sins, we have an Advocate with the Father, Jesus Christ the righteous (1 John 2:1).

What is the point of Christ's advocacy when we sin if our sins are already forgiven? He is our Advocate because new sins require new confession and new mediatorial intervention if forgiveness is to be procured. Redemption *accomplished* must be continually *applied.*

We also would point out that this is the universal experience of God's people. Our instinctive response to sin (once we see it) is confession. Granted this is not a Biblical point we are making. But the spiritual inclinations of the redeemed are not a small matter either.

3. *Recognize the damage done by sin left unconfessed.* The Bible is clear about this. Listen to Isaiah:

> Behold, the Lord's hand is not so short that it cannot save; neither is His ear so dull that it cannot hear. But your iniquities have made a separation between you and your God, and your sins have hidden His face from you, so that He does not hear. (Isa. 59:1, 2).

God is still Israel's God, Isaiah says. But your 'iniquities' have 'made a separation between you and *your* God'. There are consequences when believers sin. God at times turns His head and hides His face. He withdraws the blessed sense of His presence and refuses to hear His people's prayers. He leaves them there until they repent and turn away from their idols and lusts. This divine withdrawal has bitter consequences. David speaks of his own unconfessed sin in Psalm 32:

> When I kept silent about my sin, my body wasted away through my groaning all day long. For day and night Thy hand was heavy upon me; my vitality was drained away as with the fever heat of summer (Ps. 32:3, 4).

There are both emotional and physical consequences of unconfessed sin. He is 'groaning' all day long. God's hand is 'heavy' upon him. His energy, his 'vitality' is 'drained away' like on a hot summer day. Even his body, he says, has 'wasted away'. Only when he confessed his sin did he find relief.

> I acknowledged my sin to Thee, and my iniquity I did not hide; I said, 'I will confess my transgressions to the Lord'; and Thou didst forgive the guilt of my sin (Ps. 32:5).

David warns us ominously:

> Therefore, let everyone who is godly pray to Thee in a time when Thou mayest be found (Ps. 32:6a).

There is a time to confess sins, and it is now. We are not to toy with it. We are not to delay. Similarly David speaks of consequences in Psalm 51:

> Create in me a clean heart, O God, and renew a steadfast spirit within me. Do not cast me away from Thy presence, and do not take Thy Holy Spirit from me. Restore to me the joy of Thy salvation, and sustain me with a willing spirit (Ps. 51:10-12).

Those consequences were: his heart was corrupted (and so he pleads that God would create a new, 'clean' one in him); His character was eroded (so he prays for a renewed 'steadfast' spirit); his sense of the Spirit's presence was withdrawn ('Do not take Thy Holy Spirit from me'); and his joy was destroyed ('Restore to me the joy of my salvation'). Sin indulged and unconfessed left him compromised, broken, empty, abandoned, and grieved. Similarly in verse 8 he says:

> Make me to hear joy and gladness, let the bones which Thou hast broken rejoice. (Ps. 51:8).

'Heal my soul', the Psalmist cries, 'for I have sinned against thee' (Ps. 41:4). Fail to openly and freely acknowledge and confess your sin and you will find yourself spiritually, emotionally, and even physically imperiled. None of this is to say that you might lose your salvation, though there may be doubts raised about the salvation of a person who persists in unconfessed sin and refuses to repent. But as we've reminded ourselves, the Lord's Prayer and these Psalms are believers' prayers.

4. *Recognize the positive benefits of confession of sin.* Once confession is made and forgiveness received, then restoration occurs.

> Then I will teach transgressors Thy ways, and sinners will be converted to Thee. Deliver me from bloodguiltiness, O God, Thou God of my salvation; then my tongue will joyfully sing of Thy righteousness. O Lord, open my lips, that my mouth may declare Thy praise. For Thou dost not delight in sacrifice, otherwise I would give it; Thou art not pleased with burnt offering. The sacrifices of God are a broken spirit; a broken and a contrite heart, O God, Thou wilt not despise (Ps. 51:13-17).

Do you hear his renewed vitality and joy? He will 'teach', 'joyfully sing', and 'declare (God's) praise'. What else would we expect? *Confession is the means whereby we appropriate both the actual and psychological benefits of forgiveness.* When we confess our sins, actual forgiveness is extended, and we are 'cleansed of unrighteousness' because of what Christ has done (1 John 1:9). Through confession the healing balm of grace is applied and the wounds of sin healed. John writes:

> If we walk in the light as He Himself is in the light,
> we have fellowship with one another, and the blood
> of Jesus His Son cleanses us from all sin (1 John
> 1:7).

The benefits of the cleansing blood of Jesus are given in the context of obedience generally, ('If we walk in the light'), and confession specifically (see verses 8 and 9 above which follow in 1 John 1). From actual forgiveness flows the psychological blessings of knowing that I have 'peace' with God (Rom. 5:1; Phil. 4:9), that there is 'no condemnation' (Rom. 8:1), that I am an adopted child of God (Rom. 8:14, 15; 1 John 3:1ff). Do you lack peace? Do you lack joy? Do you lack zeal and energy for the kingdom of Christ? It may be that you have not given sufficient attention to this vital matter of confession. Perhaps you have neglected to confess your sins, whether because of ignorance, negligence, or rebellion. You've papered over them and failed to acknowledge and repent properly. Consequently, you are not receiving the daily refreshing sense that your sins have been washed away, and that you have been reconciled to God. Confession is what we need. Confession of sin is an important part of daily Christian prayer.

Pray with Contrition

Second, Jesus is teaching us in this petition to pray for forgiveness with 'broken and contrite hearts'. The phrase 'broken and contrite heart' is David's in Psalm 51. It summarizes the heart attitude with which a prayer of confession is offered. The heart is broken with grief and sorrow for the offense, and is filled with remorse and shame. This principle is indicated in the Lord's Prayer in two ways.

1. Brokenness and contrition are indicated by the use of the word 'debts'. In one sense it is being used synonymously with the word 'sin'. Indeed the term used in the parallel account of the Lords' Prayer in Luke is 'sins' (*hamartia*).

And forgive us our sins, for we ourselves also forgive everyone who is indebted to us (Luke 11:4).

Likewise, the word used when the principle is repeated in Matthew 6:14-15 is 'transgression' (*paraptoma*).

For if you forgive men for their transgressions, your heavenly Father will also forgive you. But if you do not forgive men, then your Father will not forgive your transgressions (Matt. 6:14, 15).

What the word 'debts' highlights is sin as a failed obligation owed to God, 'unpaid debts' (Packer, 161), or 'failures to render to God His lawful due' which only He can remit (Pink, 112). The word is used of monetary debts (Matt. 18:24) and metaphorically of various obligations. Obedience, service, and worship are owed to God. Whenever we fail in these areas, whenever we fail to give God what we owe to Him, we incur debts which we cannot pay. 'We have misused God's world, misapplied His good gifts, withheld service owed', says E. M. Blaiklock (41). Consequently, we fall under the penalties which the law stipulates for debtors who cannot pay their debts. This is illustrated in the parable of the Unmerciful Servant in Matthew 18:21-31. The debt owed is 10,000 times a worker's daily wage. It is unpayable.

The outlook, then, of one who seeks forgiveness is

that of one who knows that He has sinned primarily against God, and is aware of the enormity of the offense. It is God's law that has been broken; God's name that has been dishonored; God's rule that has been challenged; and God's judgment that will be borne.

'Against Thee, Thee only, I have sinned, and done what is evil in Thy sight' (Ps. 51:4).

There is implied in the word 'debts' a significant awareness of the magnitude of sin and guilt. Sin is against God. Sin incurs a debt we cannot pay, a burden we cannot lift. 'It is a bold fact that we are not Christians in the New Testament sense of the word', says Blaiklock, 'unless we have frankly faced our spiritual bankruptcy, our helplessness, and our complete unworthiness' (42).

2. *Brokenness and contrition are indicated by the second clause of the petition, 'as we forgive our debtors'.* Forgive us, in other words, in the same way that we forgive others their offenses. It is curious to find this in the middle of the prayer, especially since the principles involved are repeated in verses 14 and 15. *There* Jesus underscores the importance of forgiving others. *Here* he emphasizes the quality of the prayer that is offered. *It is the prayer of one who has a forgiving spirit.* Who has such a forgiving spirit? Only those who know the darkness of their own hearts and the magnitude of the debts for which *they* have been forgiven. Morris points out that this qualification should be seen as 'an aspiration rather than a limitation', since all forgiveness is imperfect (147). Calvin says 'it was not Christ's intention to indicate a cause, but only to tell us the attitude we should have towards our

brothers in the process of desiring to be reconciled with God'. It is designed 'to prevent anyone daring to approach God to seek forgiveness without being quite free and clear of hatred' (I, 212). 'This is not a matter of earning forgiveness by works', adds Packer, 'but of qualifying for it by repentance' (163). The attitude which grants forgiveness is the same as that which makes it possible to receive it. Those who have been broken by and forgiven of their own sins freely extend forgiveness to others. The prayer of confession that is received by God is one that comes from a heart that forgives, and no other. 'God forgives only the penitent', says Stott, and 'one of the chief evidences of true penitence is a forgiving spirit' (149).

Why is it that only those who forgive qualify for forgiveness? Because only those who understand the darkness of their own hearts and the vast proportions of their own debts are quick to forgive others theirs. Stott continues:

> Once our eyes have been opened to see the enormity of our offense against God, the injuries which others have done to us appear by comparison extremely trifling (150).

Conversely, those who cannot or will not forgive cannot truly be penitent. They cannot truly understand their own hearts or their own offenses. They minimize their own sins and exaggerate those of others. This is not a heart that is truly repentant. The parable of the 'Unmerciful Servant' concludes:

> Then summoning him, his lord said to him, 'You wicked slave, I forgave you all that debt because you entreated me. Should you not also have had

mercy on your fellow slave, even as I had mercy on you?' (Matt. 18:32, 33).

Those who are penitent are merciful. 'Should you not also have had mercy on your fellow slave, even as I had mercy on you?' *Those who have received mercy are merciful.* This is the point of the parable. We are all meant to gasp in astonishment that one who had been forgiven so much debt could be so utterly without mercy toward one who owed him such a small debt. The incongruity seems impossible to us. 'How could he?' we would ask.

Consequently, the prayer of confession which Jesus commends is one which arises from a broken and contrite heart. A heart which is profoundly aware of the enormity of its debts to God is merciful in its dealings with others.

Remember the Lord's Prayer is a type of prayer that is prayed each day. 'Give us *this* day'. Along with everything else we ask for in prayer, we are to acknowledge our sinful debts to God each day and ask for forgiveness. This means that normally we will pray not just a sentence (though because this is a *form* of prayer as well as a *pattern* it is valid to merely repeat Jesus' words) but *an extended prayer of confession*. There will arise from a contrite and broken heart a careful, detailed and extended confession of sin.

Let us summarize the qualities of a penitential prayer such as this.

1. *The truly penitent look upon their sins with grief and hatred.* We will see them as unpayable debts to our gracious and great God. We will mourn that we have

offended Him; that we have broken His good laws;
that we have fallen short of His glory; that we have
dishonored His name; that we have grieved His Holy
Spirit. We will sense the vast scope of our offenses and
be burdened by it. This is how the godly pray
throughout Scripture. The Psalmist says:

> There is no soundness in my flesh because of Thine
> indignation; there is no health in my bones because
> of my sin. For my iniquities are gone over my head;
> as a heavy burden they weigh too much for me
> (Ps. 38:3, 4).

His 'iniquities' are a 'heavy burden', he says. They have
'gone over my head'. They 'weigh too much for me'.
Again he says,

> For I know my transgressions, and my sin is ever
> before me (Ps. 51:3).

He doesn't make a quick confession and then move
on. His sin is 'ever before (him)'. It is a profoundly
disturbing and persistent burden to him.

Daniel prays a lengthy prayer of confession preceded
by 'prayer and supplications, with fastings, sackcloth,
and ashes' (Dan. 9:3). His confession is passionate and
full of grief. 'O Lord, hear! O Lord, forgive! O Lord,
listen and take action!' (Dan. 9:19).

When Ezra hears the report of Israel's sin, he writes:

> And when I heard about this matter, I tore my
> garment and my robe, and pulled some of the hair
> from my head and my beard, and sat down appalled
> (Ezra 9:3).

We read on:

> But at the evening offering I arose from my
> humiliation, even with my garment and my robe
> torn, and I fell on my knees and stretched out my
> hands to the Lord my God; and I said, 'O my God,
> I am ashamed and embarrassed to lift up my face
> to Thee, my God, for our iniquities have risen
> above our heads, and our guilt has grown even to
> the heavens' (Ezra 9:5, 6).

For Ezra, an awareness of sin results in profound
expressions of grief, sorrow, and humiliation. The
nation's guilt, it seems to him, is piled 'even to the
heavens', so vast is its scale.

As we turn to the New Testament we see more of
the same. Jesus said, 'blessed are those who mourn'
(i.e. for their sins)[1] (Matt. 5:4). He commended the
weeping of the woman in the city who 'wet His feet
with her tears, and kept wiping them with the hair of
her head' (Luke 7:38-50). He commended the publican
who prayed:

> ... unwilling to lift up his eyes to heaven, but was
> beating his breast, saying, 'God, be merciful to me,
> the sinner!' (Luke 18:13).

This unwillingness to look up, according to Morris,
'was a mark of recognition of personal unworthiness'
(*The Gospel According to John*, 635). The Apostle Paul's
self-examination results in the mighty wrestlings found
in Romans 7, the verdict, 'For I know that nothing
good dwells in me', and the climactic cry:

---

[1] see *When Grace Transforms*, 37-55

Wretched man that I am! Who will set me free from the body of this death? (Rom. 7:24).

'Oh my black Soul', cried John Donne in his second Holy Sonnet. The mature Christian is one who knows personal wretchedness. The Apostle Paul rebukes the Corinthian response to sin (or lack thereof) saying:

And you have become arrogant, and have not mourned instead, in order that the one who had done this deed might be removed from your midst (1 Cor. 5:2).

Mourning, in other words, would have been the appropriate response to the evil deed committed by one of their own. Later he commends the sorrow that led them to repentance.

For the sorrow that is according to the will of God produces a repentance without regret, leading to salvation; but the sorrow of the world produces death. For behold what earnestness this very thing, this godly sorrow, has produced in you: what vindication of yourselves, what indignation, what fear, what longing, what zeal, what avenging of wrong! In everything you demonstrated yourselves to be innocent in the matter (2 Cor. 7:10, 11).

True repentance always includes 'earnestness' and 'godly sorrow'. James describes it in this way:

Draw near to God and He will draw near to you. Cleanse your hands, you sinners; and purify your hearts, you double-minded. Be miserable and mourn and weep; let your laughter be turned into mourning, and your joy to gloom. Humble yourselves in the presence of the Lord, and He will exalt you (Jas. 4:8-10).

This is strong language. We are to be 'miserable' and 'mourn' and 'weep'. We may not be accustomed to thinking in these terms. But when we 'draw near' to a holy God, we become keenly aware of our own corruption, of our need to 'cleanse' our hands and 'purify' our hearts. The sense of sin, rightly perceived and understood, results in misery and mourning and gloom. When we see our holy God upon His throne and hear the seraphim crying out 'Holy, Holy, Holy', we cry out, 'Woe is me, for I am ruined'.

> Because I am a man of unclean lips, and I live among a people of unclean lips; for my eyes have seen the King, the Lord of hosts (Isa. 6:5).

Why is there this grief? There is a very simple answer. It is because we are dealing with a Person. God is not a Forgiveness Machine. We don't merely plug in our liturgical chant, 'Forgive me for any sins', and out pops forgiveness. Real confession involves sorrow or it is probably not real.

Consider the human parallel. When you have wronged your child or spouse, and you truly see the harm you have done, the damage to their lives, the burden to their hearts, and you truly see your fault in the matter and have quit making excuses, grief floods the soul. I remember once when Emily and I were first married and we were having an argument. I was going on relentlessly when suddenly she burst into tears and began to cry like a little girl. I had won ... but I had lost. I couldn't savor the victory. In the next instant I saw what a scoundrel I had been, what a fool, what an insensitive bully, and remorse flooded my soul. I could not move quickly enough to repent, to confess, to make right, to make restitution in all manner of ways, including notes and flowers. This is how we behave when we are dealing with a person. We don't merely say, quickly and superficially, 'I'm sorry', and move on. Not when we are dealing with a person and we mean it. By the way, if you deal with people in such ways your relationships will be superficial and strained, if not a complete mess. Do you realize that God is a person, a *divine* person, but a person nonetheless? Are you dealing with Him as a person? Or as a machine? If you are relating to God as a person you will see your sins as enormous debts owed to a good and gracious and loving Person, and *daily* grieve over and mourn your wretched and inexcusable behavior.

2. The *truly penitent will pray comprehensively and specifically.* This is the point at which many err. They will settle for generalized prayers of the 'God bless the whole world' variety. 'Forgive me for all my sins', they will parrot. The problem is that the devil is in the details, and so is forgiveness and relief. Do not settle for a *slight* healing of the wounds of sin. Don't listen to those who say, 'Peace, peace', but there is no peace' (Jer. 6:14; cf 8:11). Generalized confessions will do little to remove guilt and cleanse the conscience, any more than an adulterous man's offense is removed or his conscience relieved by a bland, 'Honey, I've not been the husband I should have been'. This is not the route to reconciliation or peace of heart. The *Westminster Confession of Faith* (in its extraordinary wisdom) counsels that we repent of sins with specificity:

> Men ought not to content themselves with a general repentance, but it is every man's duty to endeavor to repent of his particular sins, particularly (XV.5).

'Particular sins' are to be repented of 'particularly'.

One of the means that God used to awaken me to a deeper awareness of His holiness and my comparative corruption was an old historic confession of sin. While I was at Trinity College in Bristol, England, back in 1977–79, I used the *Book of Common Prayer's* 'General Confession' daily.

> Almighty and most merciful Father, we have erred and strayed from Thy ways, like lost sheep. We have followed too much the devices and desires of our own hearts. We have offended against Thy holy laws. We have left undone those things which we ought to have done, and we have done those things which we ought not to have done, and there is no health in us. But thou, O Lord, have mercy upon us miserable offenders. Spare Thou them, O God, which confess their faults. Restore Thou them that be penitent, according to Thy promises declared unto mankind, in Christ Jesus our Lord. And Grant, O most merciful Father, for His sake, that we may hereafter live a godly, righteous, and sober life, to the glory of Thy holy name.

Look at the richness of the language and imagery. Notice also its comprehensiveness. We are 'lost sheep'. We have followed the 'devices and desires of our own hearts', we have broken God's 'holy laws'. There are those things that we have left 'undone', and those things that we have done. There is 'no health in us'. We are 'miserable offenders'. Then follow the pleas for forgiveness. This prayer made an impression over time. I came to see that my personal awareness of sin was shallow, superficial, and immature.

The Prayer Book's prayer of confession used for

communion was even more impressive. At our church we use an adapted form of it on Sunday nights:

> Almighty God, Father of our Lord Jesus Christ, Maker of all things, Judge of all men; we acknowledge that we were conceived and born in iniquity, and mourn our manifold sins and wickedness, which we, from time to time, most grievously have committed, by thought, word, and deed, against Your Divine Majesty, provoking most justly Your wrath and indignation against us. We do earnestly repent, and are heartily sorry for these our misdoings; the remembrance of them is grievous unto us; the burden of them is intolerable. Have mercy upon us, most merciful Father; for Your Son our Lord Jesus Christ's sake, forgive us all that is past; And grant that we may hereafter serve and please You in newness of life, to the honour and glory of Your name; through Jesus Christ our Lord. Amen (*Leading in Worship*, 61).

Again, note how comprehensive the prayer is. We confess our *original* sin ('conceived and born in iniquity'), and our *actual sins*. They have been committed in 'thought, word and deed'. They have been 'grievously' committed against God's 'Divine Majesty'. 'Earnestly' we repent. We are 'heartily sorry'. The thought of them is 'grievous'. The 'burden' is 'intolerable'. Later editions of the Prayer Book have edited out some of this language, in particular, this notion of an 'intolerable' burden. Father William Ralston, Rector Emeritus at St John's Episcopal Church in Savannah, has said a number of times that the Episcopal church began really to be in trouble when the burden of sin ceased to be 'intolerable'.

This, of course, is a public prayer, and so lacks some specificity. But its comprehension and urgency are impressive. What is true of the confessions of sin found in the *Book of Common Prayer* is true of all the public confessions of the Reformation Era. In our book *Leading in Worship* one may find not only the two cited above (133 & 61), but also those of Calvin, Knox, Baxter, and the Westminster Directory (122, 127, 146-47, 141-42). In *The Family Worship Book* we included a condensed version of Isaac Watt's *A Guide to Prayer*, in which he teaches us to confess our sins as follows:

Of original sin and actual sins

We mourn before God because of our pride and vanity of mind, the violence of our passions, our earthly-mindedness and love of this world, our sensuality and indulgence of our flesh, our carnal security and unthankfulness under plentiful mercies, and our fretfulness and impatience, or sinful defection in a time of trouble: Our neglect of duty and want of love to God, our unbelief and hardness of heart, our slothfulness and decay in religion, the dishonors we have brought to God, and all our miscarriages towards our fellow-creatures. How often they have been repeated even before and since we knew God savingly; that we have committed them against much light; and that we have sinned against much love; and that after many rebukes of the word and providence, and many consolations from the gospel and Spirit of God. *We are ashamed, and blush to lift our faces before You our God, for our iniquities are increased over our head, and our trespasses grown up to the heavens. Behold we are vile, what shall we answer You? We will lay our hands upon our mouth, and put our mouth in the dust if so be there may hope.*

Of our deserving punishment and unworthiness of mercy

We deserve, O Lord, to be forever cast out of Your presence, and to be eternally cut off from all hope of mercy. We deserve to fall under the curse of that law which we have broken, and to be forever banished from the blessings of the gospel which we have so long refused. We have sinned against so much mercy, *that we are no longer worthy to be called Your children.* We are utterly unworthy of any of those favors that are promised in Your word, and which you have given us encouragement to hope for. *If You contend with us for our transgressions, we are not able to answer You, O Lord, nor do we make excuse for one of a thousand, if You should mark our iniquities, O Lord, who shall stand? But there is forgiveness with You, there is mercy and plenteous redemption'* (p. 99).

I especially love his confession that we have sinned even 'since we've come to know Christ savingly', sinning 'against much light; and ... against much love', even 'after many rebukes of the word and providence, and many consolations from the gospel and Spirit of God'. The prayer is comprehensive, specific, and passionate.

I cite one final example, that of the Presbyterian Matthew Henry, whose *Commentary on the Whole Bible* is the most beloved and widely used of all Bible commentaries. He also wrote *A Method for Prayer.* His prayer of confession is divided into 11 sections, one of which is further divided into 6 additional sections, the whole continuing for a total of 21 pages! We should note that his 'Petitions and Supplications' section lasts 36 pages and thanksgivings lasts 32 pages, so confession is not disproportionate, just thorough – exceedingly thorough.

If someone is tempted to say that these are merely human authorities that we are citing, then again I commend to them Psalm 51. Follow the personal pronoun as David owns his culpability for his sin and pleads for forgiveness and cleansing:

> Be gracious to me, O God, according to Thy lovingkindness; according to the greatness of Thy compassion blot out my transgressions. Wash me thoroughly from my iniquity, and cleanse me from my sin. For I know my transgressions, and my sin is ever before me. Against Thee, Thee only, I have sinned, and done what is evil in Thy sight .... Behold, I was brought forth in iniquity, and in sin my mother conceived me .... Purify me with hyssop, and I shall be clean; wash me, and I shall be whiter than snow. Make me to hear joy and gladness, let the bones which Thou hast broken rejoice. Hide Thy face from my sins, and blot out all my iniquities .... Deliver me from bloodguiltiness, O God, Thou God of my salvation; then my tongue will joyfully sing of Thy righteousness' (Ps. 51:1-4a, 5, 7-9, 14).

David goes back to original sin ('in sin my mother conceived me'), internal or heart sins ('Behold Thou dost desire truth in the innermost being'), guilt and other consequences. He does not settle for a mere 'Forgive me for all of my sins'. He searches himself comprehensively; thoughts and deeds, heart and actions.

Similarly, Daniel in his ninth chapter confesses the sins of the nation of Israel using comprehensive terminology to do so. They had 'sinned, committed iniquity, acted wickedly, and rebelled, even turning aside' from God's commandments (Dan. 9:5). His confession continues for sixteen verses and implicates the kings, princes, fathers, and the whole people. Why are David and Daniel comprehensive in their confessions? Because they want to make it right. They are dealing with a Person. Because confession is the means by which we appropriate forgiveness, the more thorough one's self-examination and confession, the more fully forgiveness, restoration, peace, and joy are experienced.

Pray with Confidence

Third, we conclude our contemplation of this expression of confession with a reminder. *We pray with the confidence that as we confess our sins with contrition and sincerity, God forgives our sins and cleanses our hearts.* This is the promise of the fifth petition. Jesus died for sins. Atonement has been made. Forgiveness is promised to all who will acknowledge their sins. The question that remains is, are we confessing our sins? Or have we failed to search our souls, leaving whole areas of life unexamined and uncleansed? Have we settled for superficial and inadequate confession, never really dealing with the issues of life before God? What about our thoughts? What about our hearts? our pride? our self-righteousness? our hypocrisy? our judgementalism? our envy and jealousy and covetousness? What about our words? our harsh rebukes of others? our sarcasm? our vulgarity? our suggestive and untoward comments? What about our deeds? How do we treat our spouses? our children? our neighbors? our employer or employees? our brothers and sisters in Christ? How do we respond to God? His grace? His love? His kindness to us? His Word? His law? His Bride the church?

How do you stack up? Most of us don't at all. We fall far short. We miserably fail to be what we should be and do what we should do. As we examine ourselves at this level we will find rottenness and corruption. It is not easy to look at. We may be tempted to avert our gaze, to not go there, and remain comfortable and content with ourselves. But as we openly acknowledge our debts to God, He promises to forgive them all. This is the gospel. Christ bore our sins in His body (1 Pet. 2:24). He became a 'curse' for us (Gal. 3:13). He gave His life as a 'ransom' for ours (Mark 10:45). He who knew no sin became sin that we might receive God's righteousness in Him (2 Cor. 5:21). Our iniquities have been laid upon Him (Is. 53:11). This is how we are saved and how we change. This is how we stir up a healthy discontent with our current spiritual condition and press on to greater depth and maturity. All that is required of us is the humility to openly confess our sins to God, and the blood of Christ cleanses. He pardons our offenses. He remits our debts. He changes our hearts.

11

Lead us Not Into Temptation

The sixth and final petition flows naturally from the fifth. I have come to God with my sins. I have learned to view them as 'debts' incurred by failed obligations to love, serve, and obey God. I grasp the magnitude of those debts. They are far beyond my ability to pay. The seriousness of the situation is impressed upon me. I see the darkness of my own soul and the corruption of my own heart. I know what I deserve. Yet Christ gave His life as a 'ransom' for mine (Mark 10:45). He rescued me from the debtor's prison. He redeemed me from bondage to sin (Col. 1:13,14). When He did (at conversion), and each time He does (in ongoing confession), peace and joy fill my soul. The great burden of debt and guilt are lifted. I am forgiven.

How blessed is he whose transgression is forgiven, whose sin is covered. How blessed is the man to whom the Lord does not impute iniquity, and in whose spirit there is no deceit! (Ps. 32:1, 2).

What a glorious gospel! What 'amazing grace'! What 'amazing love'! 'How can it be?' What 'amazing pity, grace unknown, and love beyond degree'. Our hymn writers, with the Biblical authors, celebrate this experience! 'Behold what manner of love the Father has given unto us' (1 John 3:1). I am overwhelmed by the sense both of my unworthiness and of the astonishing grace of God.

What is the result of this sense? That *I never want to go back there again*. Never again! May I never fall again! Never again may I submit to my lusts. Never again may my tongue wag out of control. Never again may my temper explode in profanity or violence. Never again may I indulge my spiritual pride and self-righteousness. Never again may I harden my heart to those in need.

Let me go on. What do I know as one who has received forgiveness for his debts? I know what it is like to live 'in sin'. I know the bondage, what Peter called 'the bondage of iniquity' (Acts 8:23), the oppressive, tyrannical, all-consuming slavery to an evil that I cannot control. I know what it is to say, 'I do the very thing I do not wish to do' (Rom. 7:16).

For that which I am doing, I do not understand;
for I am not practicing what I would like to do,
but I am doing the very thing I hate (Rom. 7:15).

I know the deceitfulness of my own heart (Jer. 17:9), the self-deception and delusion that evil perpetuates. I have been in the moral fog caused by sin, and have been blinded by 'the god of this world' (2 Cor. 4:4). I know what it is to be seduced by evil and enticed by abominations in the name of adventure, romance, and excitement. I know what it is to have unbridled ambition for power or fame or wealth blind me to my destructive abuse of others.

I also know the overwhelming sense of shame and sorrow that floods my soul when the fog finally lifts, and I see myself clearly. I know the grief that overwhelms when I finally realize the damage that I have done to others, even my loved ones. Finally, I know personal weakness and vulnerability. I know failure, and know that in the wrong circumstances I am likely to fail again. The devil, the flesh, and the world are too strong. So I am absolutely certain of one thing – I never want to go back there again. May I never be like those who 'are again entangled' in the 'defilements of the world'. May I never be like the dog who returns to his vomit, or like the sow who returns to wallow in the mire (2 Pet. 2:20-22). I abhor what is evil and am clinging (for dear life) to what is good (Rom. 12:9).

Consequently, I beg and plead:

> And do not lead us into temptation, but deliver us from evil (Matt. 6:13a).

What are we saying in this petition?

Dependence

First, we are acknowledging our entire dependence upon God. Packer sees one dominating thought in the two halves of this petition: 'life is a spiritual minefield: amid such dangers we dare not trust ourselves' (165). Christians, we should note, are subject to temptation's reach. When we came to Christ we did not suddenly rise above temptation's reach. We are not now immune to sin. It would be a great error to think so. The flesh remains weak so we must keep 'watching and praying' (Matt. 26:41). We are subject to the temptation to commit the whole range of human sins given the wrong circumstances. If even the man after God's own heart, the writer of so many Psalms, that great King, David, could fall, then so can we. If Judas could betray Christ and Peter could deny Christ, then so can we. We pray this prayer because we know our extreme weakness. We are utterly unable to keep ourselves from sin without the help of God. We pray this not as rank pagans, but as disciples, as believers. Even as those who are born again we must say that we sink unless God keeps us afloat, that we fall unless God makes us stand (Rom. 14:4). He is the vine and we are the branches. Only as we abide in Him can we bear fruit. 'Apart from Me', Jesus says, 'you can do nothing' (John 15:5). Our adequacy for anything is only in Christ (2 Cor. 2:16–3:5). Am I strong enough to keep myself believing? to resist the temptation of unbelief? the temptation of cynicism? of despair? of anxiety? of lust? of greed? of envy? of covetousness? No, I am not. Regeneration isn't enough. Church membership isn't enough. Even the indwelling of the Holy Spirit is not enough. God must give me the fullness of His Holy Spirit or I will fail (Eph. 5:18). He must give me the constant grace to stand or I will fall, if not today then tomorrow. I pray this prayer because I am entirely dependent upon God. Do you know this about yourself? Do you realize how weak and vulnerable you are?

> Prone to wander – Lord I feel it –
> Prone to leave the God I love:
> Here's my heart, O take and seal it,
> Seal it for Thy courts above.

Because we are 'prone to wander' we can't be arrogant about the sins and failings of others. The Apostle Paul warns:

Therefore let him who thinks he stands take heed lest he fall (1 Cor. 10:12).

Point at any particular sin and we can say, 'There but for the grace of God go I'. This is the 'weakness' to which the Apostle Paul refers, and which is so critical to the living of the Christian life. We are strong only as we realize our utter weakness and inability, and consequently put all our trust and confidence in Christ. The Apostle had his 'thorn in the flesh, a messenger of Satan'. It was a hindrance to him. It weakened him. So he prayed for deliverance, not once but three times. Yet God saw fit not to remove it. Why? Because it was performing a valuable function. Listen to him:

And He has said to me, 'My grace is sufficient for you, for power is perfected in weakness.' Most gladly, therefore, I will rather boast about my weaknesses, that the power of Christ may dwell in me. Therefore I am well content with weaknesses, with insults, with distresses, with persecutions, with difficulties, for Christ's sake; for when I am weak, then I am strong (2 Cor. 12:9, 10).

'Power is perfected in weakness', he says. 'When I am weak, then I am strong'. The awareness of weakness and consequent dependence upon God lies behind this sixth petition. This awareness drives me to my knees, keenly aware of my vulnerability, praying 'Lead me not into temptation!' 'Keep watching and praying', Jesus said, 'that you may not enter into temptation'. Why should we do that, Jesus? Because 'the spirit is willing, but the flesh is *weak*' (Matt. 26:41).

Circumstances

Second, we are acknowledging that God is the Lord of circumstances. As we have seen, He orders 'all things' after the counsel of His will (Eph. 1:11). He is able to open and close doors of opportunity (Col. 4:1-4). He is not the God of the deists – distant, remote and uninvolved. He intervenes in our lives. He is 'able to keep (us) from falling'.

> Now to Him who is able to keep you from
> stumbling, and to make you stand in the presence
> of His glory blameless with great joy (Jude 24).

He is able to cause 'all things' to work together for our good (Rom. 8:28). So Jesus teaches us to pray as follows:

1. *Lead us not into temptation.* God is able to so 'lead' or 'direct' us that we may find ourselves outside the place of temptation or testing (*peirasmos*). God Himself does not directly 'tempt' us, as James points out (Jas. 1:13). Nevertheless, He *does* allow/permit/ordain/decree/plan for us to encounter temptations/tests/trials. 'God does and must test us regularly, to prove what is in us and show how far we have got', says Packer. 'His purpose is wholly constructive' (165). The devil tests in order to destroy. God tests in order to strengthen. James writes:

> Consider it all joy, my brethren, when you
> encounter various trials, knowing that the testing
> of your faith produces endurance. And let
> endurance have its perfect result, that you may be
> perfect and complete, lacking in nothing (Jas. 1:2-
> 4).

Clearly there is value in such trials. Testing strengthens us. It 'produces endurance'. The 'various trials' of which Peter speaks result in the 'proof' of our faith (1 Pet. 1:6, 7). There is value in this. We ought not to seek trials. We ought to seek the opposite. We ought to no more seek trials than a football team ought to seek close games. You learn a lot from close, hard fought games. But your aim ought to be to annihilate the opposition. A coach shouldn't say to his team, 'All right men, let's go out and play it close so that we can learn a lot'. Of course not. You play to beat the opposition on every play and win big. Again Packer says, 'Temptation may be our lot, but only a fool will make it his preference' (166). The prayer, then, is that God would protect us from tempting circumstances. What exactly constitutes tempting circumstances is going to vary from person to person. But we all have them, and it is to be our fervent prayer that God will spare us exposure to them.

a. *places* – for some, there are places they should not go. They should not go to a convenience store or on the internet because of the porn readily available. They should not go to a liquor store because of the availability of alcohol. There may be stores that arouse lust, covetousness, or discontent. We have had to cancel certain catalogs because of their erotic content. Others clearly stir up a spirit of discontent as they expose us to all the toys that we do not now possess. We are praying in this petition for God to keep us from those places where we might fall. We want nothing to do with them. We want to keep far from them, lest they once again lead us to sin against our gracious Father.

b. *persons* – for others, there are people with whom they should not associate. Paul warned 'bad company corrupts good morals' (1 Cor. 15:33). There are people with whom I am tempted to sin. There are people also who will entice me to corrupt my language (tempting me to curse or to gossip), my marriage (tempting me to violate my vows), or the requirements of moderation (tempting me to eat or drink excessively). Keep far from them. Do you become cruel or mean or arrogant when with them? Don't go near them. Do they cause you to stumble? Do they lead you into sin? Some people encourage godliness. Some people lift us to Christ. Others tear us down. Seek out the former but avoid the latter. Lead us not into temptation.

c. *products* – There are products which in themselves are a snare for us. Some foods entice us to gluttony. The television or Internet may tempt us to waste time. The world offers 'the lust of the eyes', that is, the beautiful and wonderful things that easily become idols (1 John 2:15, 16). Jesus warned of the 'deceitfulness of riches' (Matt. 13:22). There are things, often not evil in themselves, that for us, because of obsessiveness, become idols.

We are praying in this petition that God will keep us from all circumstances wherein we might succumb to temptation. If I lack Joseph's strength, keep me from Potiphar's wife (Gen. 39). If I am vulnerable to the flesh like David, keep me from Bathsheba (2 Sam. 11). If I am a coward when persecuted, keep me from circumstances like Peter's on the night of Jesus' betrayal (Matt. 26:69-75). If I covet riches, keep me from opportunities such as Elisha's servant Gehazi experienced (2 Kgs. 5). If the good opinion of others is a snare to me, keep me from opportunities to deceive like those encountered by Ananias and Sapphira (Acts 5). If authority and position is important to me, then keep me from the course of Diotrephes, 'who loveth to be preeminent' (3 John 9). If I am tempted to love the world, keep me from the path of Demas, who 'having loved this present world' deserted Paul (2 Tim. 4:10). This prayer is the prayer of the humble. It is the prayer of those who know how vulnerable they are. We remind ourselves, again, that we pray this way because we live this way. We are eager to live holy lives. We hunger and thirst after righteousness. Consequently, we not only *pray* for deliverance, but we ourselves actually *flee* from sin (1 Cor. 6:18, 1 Tim. 6:11). We want nothing to do with it. We keep far from it.

2. *Deliver us from evil* – 'If (disciples) do find themselves in such a (tempting) situation', says France, 'they must pray to be delivered *from evil*' (136). The *Shorter Catechism* understands the sixth petition to mean 'that God would either keep us from being tempted to sin', or, in this second part of it, 'support and deliver us when we are tempted' (Q. 106). The commentators go back and forth over whether or not it should be rendered 'evil' or 'evil one' (there is no definite article). Following Morris, it seems to me that the traditional rendering, 'evil' is still to be preferred. But the meaning is not significantly altered either way. This is a cry for rescue. I am now actually in the tempting circumstances. God has seen fit to allow me into this tempting and testing situation. Now what do I pray? Rescue me! Save me! Deliver me from this test which I must pass!

The evil circumstances in which we find ourselves could include attacks by the 'evil one'. Is there a devil? The Bible testifies that there are both demons and a prince among them, 'Satan' (Greek *Satanas*), meaning 'adversary'. The 'tempter' attacked and tempted Jesus in the wilderness, furiously assaulting Him in His places of need (e.g. food and faith – Matt. 4:1-11). When the devil left, he left only 'for a season', and 'until an opportune time' (Luke 4:13). His opposition to us is ferocious, like that of a 'roaring lion ... seeking whom he may devour' (1 Pet. 5:8). Yet he 'disguises himself as an angel of light' and his servants 'disguise themselves as servants of righteousness' (2 Cor. 11:14, 15). The devil can come after us in every way, as horrid evil, or dressed up as something good, beautiful, and wonderful. Paul speaks of the 'schemes' of the devil (Eph. 6:11). He speaks of the 'struggle' in which we are engaged, not against 'flesh and blood', but:

> ... against the rulers, against the powers, against the world forces of this darkness, against the spiritual forces of wickedness in the heavenly places (Eph. 6:12b).

Consequently, we can know that assaults will come, and we need protection.

> Therefore, take up the full armor of God, that you may be able to resist in the evil day, and having done everything, to stand firm (Eph. 6:13).

There comes for us all an 'evil day' which we must 'resist' and against which we must 'stand firm'. Satan comes perhaps as he did to Jesus in the wilderness, firing all his artillery at once in an attempt to bring us down. Yet he may do so disguised as something good. How are we delivered from such evil? By the 'full armor of

God'. He strengthens us. He shields us. The devil has his 'snare' (1 Tim. 3:7). Finally some are overcome and 'held captive by him to do his will' (2 Tim. 2:26). He is a brute, he is relentless. And he is cunning. When we give sin a place in our lives, he takes 'advantage' of it, and 'schemes' to achieve our destruction (2 Cor. 2:11). Don't give him an 'opportunity' (Eph. 4:27). He would like to 'sift' us 'like wheat' (Luke 22:31). He seeks to tempt us with the aim of destroying us (1 Cor. 7:5).

The devil may be resisted (1 Pet. 5:9; Jas. 4:7). He is a defeated enemy. He will flee! One of the ways to resist him, as Paul says, is to not be 'ignorant' of his schemes (2 Cor. 2:11). Know his subtlety. Don't look for a ridiculous figure with horns and a pointed tail. More typically he comes mingled with much good. He comes as an 'angel of light'. Good things are happening through his agents and programs. Positive things. But he has gotten you off track. You are looking in the wrong direction. You are using the wrong means. It may even seem like a divine provision. But it has compromised you, and you know it. The devil has outmaneuvered you. You are thinking of how much this helps you, or your family, or your work. But you're off track, and as time passes he pushes you further and further off track until a small, seemingly 'harmless' sin has grown to such proportions that it may destroy your whole life. I know of a minister who while traveling across country to serve a missions board fell into an affair with a woman not his wife. I know of another who, while staying up late to complete a commentary on Mark's gospel, had an affair with his typist. His foreward refers cryptically to how much the work on his commentary had cost his wife and children. How does this happen? It is the work of the deceiver. He schemes our fall. He schemes, and attacks our weakness. What can we do? At the first notice begin to pray, 'Deliver me from evil. Help me to see through this and escape it. Help me to see this for what it really is, and not to be seduced or deluded'.

We need not ultimately fear the devil. Jesus came to destroy his works (1 John 3:8). He 'rendered powerless' the devil (Heb. 2:14). The fury with which we are dealing is the rage of a dying enemy. He will soon be crushed under our feet (Rom. 16:20).

The Apostle Paul could claim with confidence:

> The Lord will deliver me from every evil deed, and will bring me safely to His heavenly kingdom; to Him be the glory forever and ever. Amen (2 Tim. 4:18).

Similarly he writes:

> No temptation has overtaken you but such as is common to man; and God is faithful, who will not allow you to be tempted beyond what you are able, but with the temptation will provide the way of escape also, that you may be able to endure it (1 Cor. 10:13).

All of our temptations are 'common'. None of them is exceptional. A believer can never say, 'I was confronted with an extraordinary temptation beyond my capacity for resistance'. It cannot happen, at least not in this sense. Our temptations are never beyond that which a born-again and Spirit-indwelt believer can resist. Greater is He who is in us than he who is in the world (1 John 4:4). If temptation becomes too much, God provides 'a way of escape' so that we are 'able to endure it'.

How does He deliver us?

i) by strengthening us to overcome the temptation;
ii) by removing the tempting circumstance from us;
iii) by removing us from the tempting circumstance.

The classic example is Joseph with Potiphar's wife.
Joseph knew that he could not stay where he was, with
Potiphar's wife grasping lustfully at him. He fled! (Gen.
39:12). That was his way of escape. It was to flee with
all his might! There are times when we must simply,
and quite literally, flee. As Luther says, we cannot keep
the birds from flying over our heads, but we can keep
them from building nests in our hair. Temptations will
come. Our responsibility is to forsake them when they
do. 'Better shun the bait', said Dryden, 'than struggle
in the snare' (Blaiklock, 55).

On other occasions, God may remove the tempting
circumstance. He may strike the tempting person. He
may destroy the tempting place or product. At other
times God may remove us. This sounds ominous, and
sometimes it is. He may use sickness or accidents, or
even death, to remove the occasion of temptation. But
even this would be acceptable to us because we so hate
evil, and so want to resist it that we become willing to
undergo whatever it takes to avoid it.

We pray this prayer, then, as those who are zealous
to live holy lives. We can't bear the thought of sinning
against the love and grace of a holy Father.
Consequently, it is our passionate prayer that we will
not be led into temptation, that we will be delivered
from evil and the evil one.

IV

The Benediction and Plea

12

The Kingdom, Power, and Glory

We come now to the final sentence of this great prayer, the model prayer, the Lord's Prayer. It is classified as the third section of the prayer, after the preface and petitions. Again we remind ourselves of the structure:

Preface of praise: 'Our Father who art in heaven'

Six Petitions: 'Hallowed be Thy name. Thy kingdom come. Thy will be done, On earth as it is in heaven. Give us this day our daily bread. And forgive us our debts, as we also have forgiven our debtors. And do not lead us into temptation, but deliver us from evil'.

Benediction and Plea: 'For Thine is the kingdom, the power, and the glory, forever. Amen.'

The prayer concludes with a doxology, an ascription of praise that is at the same time a plea to be heard and answered. Many questions are raised about the authenticity of these words. They are missing from the oldest New Testament manuscripts. Packer's comment: its 'not the best manuscripts. Nevertheless, it is in the best tradition!' (175). But there is also considerable early support for their inclusion in the original text, and at least one modern scholar has argued vigorously for this view (W. D. Davies, *The Setting of the Sermon on the Mount*, pp. 451-453). Because the tradition of inclusion goes back so far (it is referred to in the *Didache* and the *Apostolic Constitutions*), and because it has been regarded by the church as Scripture for so long, I believe that we are wise to treat it as part of the original text, following our normal course of interpretation and application. How are we to regard these words?

Pleading with God

First, the concluding doxology is a plea. 'For' (*hoti*) means 'because'. The sense is 'here's why You should hear my prayer'. It is 'a plea and argument to enforce the petitions', says Pink (130). Hear me *because* Yours is the kingdom, power, and glory. Hallow Your name, bring about Your kingdom, do Your will, give us bread, forgive our debts, and lead and deliver us *because* to You belongs the rule, the power, and the glory. It is an argument as to why the Father ought to answer the prayer. Jesus is presenting reasons 'drawn from the Divine perfections', says Pink, as to why the Father ought to be willing and able to grant His requests (133).

The notion of pleading in prayer has been lost on most believers these days, but the Bible is full of the pleas of God's people. Isaac Watts in his *Guide to Prayer* includes 'Pleading, or arguing our case with Him in a fervent, yet humble manner' as a category of prayer, indeed his longest category, along with Invocation, Adoration, Confession, Petition, Self-dedication, Thanksgiving, and Benediction. He divides our 'pleadings' into seven different categories. He bases them upon the following biblical categories:

1. The greatness of our needs (we are so poor, so weak, so destitute, etc.)
2. The perfections of God's nature (because He is all powerful, all wise, and all good)
3. The various relations in which God stands to us (is He not our Father, our Maker, our King?)
4. The promises of the covenant of grace (have You not said? have You not promised? Remember Your covenant!)
5. The name and honor of God (what will unbelievers think if You do not act?)
6. The former experiences of others and ourselves (remember how You delivered people in times past)
7. The name and meditation of our Lord Jesus Christ (we are 'in Christ', and remember what He has done for us, remember His suffering, and His triumph. Be pleased to hear us even as You are pleased to hear Him) (Watts, 20-26).

On the basis of these sorts of things we make our case to God in prayer. We see this again and again from the saints of old. Job, for example, says:

I would present my case before Him and fill my mouth with arguments (Job 23:4).

This seems to indicate that we may present *our* case to God. We have the liberty in prayer to 'fill (our) mouth(s) with arguments'. We must do so reverently, and Job at times approaches irreverence. Still, God is pleased to hear our arguments when presented in 'a fervent, yet humble manner' (Watts, 20).

Abraham appealed to the justice of God as he pleaded for the sparing of Sodom and Gomorrah.

> And Abraham came near and said, 'Wilt Thou indeed sweep away the righteous with the wicked? Suppose there are fifty righteous within the city; wilt Thou indeed sweep it away and not spare the place for the sake of the fifty righteous who are in it? Far be it from Thee to do such a thing, to slay the righteous with the wicked, so that the righteous and the wicked are treated alike. Far be it from Thee! Shall not the Judge of all the earth deal justly?' (Gen. 18:23-25).

Do you see the basis for his repeated appeal? Why should God spare Sodom? Because fairness may demand it. A just God would not 'sweep away the righteous with the wicked' (v. 23). He would not 'slay the righteous with the wicked, so that the righteous and the wicked are treated alike'. Listen to him plead. 'Far be it from Thee! Lord God you could not do such a thing! Shall not the judge of all the earth deal justly?' (v. 25). Abraham is humble about it:

> And Abraham answered and said, 'Now behold, I have ventured to speak to the Lord, although I am but dust and ashes' (Gen. 18:27).

He is humble. He is but 'dust and ashes'. But he is also insistent and bold.

Then he said, 'Oh may the Lord not be angry, and
I shall speak only this once; suppose ten are found
there?' And He said, 'I will not destroy it on
account of the ten' (Gen. 18:32).

One might have thought that it was impertinent to
speak to God in this way. But apparently this is not so.
The saints of old regularly plead with God. Why would
we pray with pleadings? 'It is our duty to plead with
God in prayer', says Matthew Henry, 'to fill our mouth
with arguments (Job 23:4) not to move God, but to
affect ourselves; to encourage our faith, to excite our
fervency, and to evidence both'. We plead, in other
words, so as to build our own trust and confidence and
urgency, because believing prayers are the only kind that
God answers. We are not trying to change God, rather to
change ourselves, from a condition of unbelief,
lethargy, and doubt, to one of faith, zeal, and trust.

Not only Abraham, but Moses also pleads with God.
On the occasion of the idolatrous worship of the golden
calf, God threatened to destroy the whole nation of
Israel. But Moses began to plead for the people:

Then Moses entreated the Lord his God, and said,
'O Lord, why doth Thine anger burn against Thy
people whom Thou hast brought out from the land
of Egypt with great power and with a mighty hand?
Why should the Egyptians speak, saying, "With
evil intent He brought them out to kill them in
the mountains and to destroy them from the face
of the earth"? Turn from Thy burning anger and
change Thy mind about doing harm to Thy people.
Remember Abraham, Isaac, and Israel, Thy
servants to whom Thou didst swear by Thyself,
and didst say to them, "I will multiply your

descendants as the stars of the heavens, and all this land of which I have spoken I will give to your descendants, and they shall inherit it forever"' (Exod. 32:11-13).

Moses appeals to God's prior works (32:11), His reputation among the nations (v. 12), and His covenant with Abraham and prior promise (v. 13). Did You not already bring this people out of Egypt 'with great power and with a mighty hand?'. If you destroy Your people won't the Egyptians impugn your motives saying, 'with evil intent He brought them out to kill them?' What about your covenant? 'Remember Abraham, Isaac, and Israel' to whom You made Your promises. The result of his pleas?

So the Lord changed His mind about the harm which He said He would do to His people. (Ex. 32:14) (cf 33:12-16; Deut. 9:18-20). This kind of prayer is effectual.

David's urgent pleadings may be found throughout the Psalms. One example:

Contend, O Lord, with those who contend with me; fight against those who fight against me. Take hold of buckler and shield, and rise up for my help. Draw also the spear and the battle-axe to meet those who pursue me; say to my soul, 'I am your salvation'. Let those be ashamed and dishonored who seek my life; let those be turned back and humiliated who devise evil against me. Let them be like chaff before the wind, with the angel of the Lord driving them on. Let their way be dark and slippery, with the angel of the Lord pursuing them. For without cause they hid their net for me; without cause they dug a pit for my soul. Let destruction come upon him unawares; and let the

net which he hid catch himself; into that very
destruction let him fall... Lord, how long wilt Thou
look on? Rescue my soul from their ravages, my
only life from the lions. I will give Thee thanks in
the great congregation; I will praise Thee among a
mighty throng. Do not let those who are
wrongfully my enemies rejoice over me; neither
let those who hate me without cause wink
maliciously. For they do not speak peace, but they
devise deceitful words against those who are quiet
in the land. And they opened their mouth wide
against me; they said, 'Aha, aha, our eyes have seen
it!' (Ps. 35:1-8, 17-21) (cf Ps. 13, 28, 35, 43, 44, 55,
57:1-3, 59, 61, 64, 80, 83, 88, 90)

Contend, fight, take hold, rise up, draw the spear and
axe, says David. Let them be ashamed, dishonored,
turned back, humiliated, and so on. Why? Because they
are wicked. Because 'without cause they hid their net
for me' (v 7). Because they 'wrongfully ... rejoice over
me'. Because they 'hate me without a cause' (v 19).
Abraham, Moses, David, and all the saints plead with
God in prayer. They reason with Him and seek to
persuade Him. So also does Jesus teach us to do so here.
Why? Because in one sense this is how we deal with
rational beings. I am sometimes amazed at how adept
my children are at arguing for some privilege they want
granted, whether it be dessert, to stay up an extra hour,
or to buy some product. They are able to marshal
arguments like a country lawyer. Our God is a personal
and rational God. He says to us, 'Come now, and let
us reason together' (Is. 1:18). Watch people at traffic
court provide reasons for reducing their fines. The same
is generally the case with those who bring reports to
the Session of the church or the board of directors of a

company. When we seek to persuade those with authority to take a given course of action, particularly when it is in our best interest for them to do so, we don't just present a list of requests. We don't just say, 'I want this, and this, and this, and this'. We provide reasons. We seek to persuade. We reason, we argue, we plead, we make our case. Likewise, this is the Biblical manner of praying. This leads to two additional points:

1. *Jesus specifically models pleading on the basis of God's self-interest.* Why should God answer our prayer? What argument do we present? We've seen a host of reasons in our samples of pleading already. But the supreme reason is God's self-interest, or to put it another way, God's own glory. Answer our prayer, O Lord, because Yours is the kingdom, power, and glory, and therefore You will benefit from the things which we seek in prayer. In other words, we are praying according to the will of God. God has a vested interest in the success of our prayer. We want and are praying for those things which God wants. Jesus taught us to pray for His kingdom to come. Does the Father have an interest in this coming about? Of course — His is the kingdom. We are reminding Him of this. Since 'Thine is the kingdom', hear our prayer that the kingdom should come. Isn't that a good argument? Doesn't this build our confidence that He will hear and grant this request? Lord, should You not cause Your kingdom to come since Yours is the kingdom?

Jesus taught us to pray for His will to be done. Since His is the kingdom, which as we have seen means that His is the *rule*, we are reminding God that this is the end toward which His rule is directed. Because 'Thine is the kingdom', grant our request that Your will be done all the time in every place. When God's kingdom is consummated, His will *will* be done completely. Why should God give us bread, forgive our debts, and deliver us from temptation and evil? Both because it will advance His kingdom and glorify Him. His is the glory. Glorify Yourself then by providing Your people who seek to serve You the things that they need. Do you see the point? Because Yours is the rule, the power, and the glory, hallow Your name, bring on Your kingdom, accomplish Your will and supply Your people with bread, forgiveness, and safe-keeping.

Typically we aim too low in the ends for which we pray. Jesus is teaching us to aim high. We don't pray for bread just to have a full stomach and personal comfort. There is nothing wrong with praying on this basis. God cares about our hunger pains, our discomfort, and our resulting weakness. But we shouldn't stop there. Ultimately we seek bread so that we might glorify God (see ch. 9). We are to glorify God 'whether we eat or drink or whatever we do' (1 Cor. 10:31). So this is the basis of my appeal to God. Lord give me bread because then I shall have bodily strength and be able to live not for myself but for You (2 Cor. 5:15). If I have no food I cannot serve you. My ministry to my children and wife, my ministry at church, my influence in the marketplace will all cease. Your kingdom will be harmed! Souls may be lost! This, by the way, will have a shaping effect on our prayers. If we conclude our prayers with sentiments such as these, we will only ask for those things that are consistent with His kingdom, power, and glory. God-centered thinking will shape our prayers and our prayers will express God-centered living. We will pray according to the will of God as we seek to live according

to the will of God. We see once more that we pray as
we live and we live as we pray. As we learn to present
our case to God, it will force us to think as God does
about these things. His agenda and priorities will be
foremost in our minds, and we will more and more
think and *live* as we are learning to *pray*.

2. Jesus is teaching us to plead on the basis of God's ability.
Is God able to do these things about which we have
prayed? Can He hallow His name, cause His kingdom
to come, and cause His will to be done on earth as in
heaven? Can He supply bread, pardon sins, and keep
us from temptation and evil? Oh, yes, He can! Why?
'For', or 'because', His is the rule (kingdom). His is
the power. He has all the authority and power of heaven
and earth. Nothing is impossible for Him. It is 'within
his *capacity* and ... in line with his character', says Packer
(175). With God all things are possible. So we are
reminding Him of this. Remember, O Lord, that You
are able to do, and do exceedingly abundant beyond
all that we can ask or think (Eph. 3:20). You can supply
our material need. You can deliver us from the burden
of sin and liberate us from our bondage to sin.
Remember what Paul said to the Corinthians:

> Or do you not know that the unrighteous shall
> not inherit the kingdom of God? Do not be
> deceived; neither fornicators, nor idolaters, nor
> adulterers, nor effeminate, nor homosexuals, nor
> thieves, nor the covetous, nor drunkards, nor
> revilers, nor swindlers, shall inherit the kingdom
> of God. And such were some of you; but you were
> washed, but you were sanctified, but you were
> justified in the name of the Lord Jesus Christ, and
> in the Spirit of our God (1 Cor. 6:9-11).

'And such were some of you'. What happened? They were delivered, washed, justified, and sanctified! God has the power. He is able to change hearts, change communities, and change nations. He can send a revival that would convert the whole world. So we remind Him – Yours is the kingdom and rule. Yours is the power. Yours is the glory. Hear our prayer and glorify Yourself by using Your great power for these great ends! This is why we don't just *say* our prayers. Rather, we labor in prayer. We work at it. We wrestle with God in prayer like Jacob with the angel of the Lord, who even though crippled refused to quit, saying, 'I will not let you go unless you bless me' (Gen. 32:26). At that point, and not before, the Angel did bless him. Jacob became a new man with a new name, 'Israel'. Jesus is teaching us to plead, to wrestle, to prevail.

Hope

Second, the concluding doxology is an expression of our hope. 'Forever', He concludes. His kingdom, power, and glory shall endure forever. His glory will never be diminished. His kingdom and power will never be overthrown. We pray always in the confidence and hope that we are on the right side of history. God's name shall be hallowed, His kingdom shall come, and His will shall be done on earth as it is in heaven. This means that there is an optimistic cast to our prayers and, by extension, to our lives. The doxology is 'a confirmation and declaration of confidence that the prayer will be heard' says Pink (130). We are often provoked by our needs to pray. Often our troubles drive us to our knees. In this sense we are realistic in ways that unbelievers are afraid to be. They often want to assume an optimistic outlook, but do so with no basis. They pretend. It doesn't really hurt! Ignore the pain and look on the bright side! Then it will all go away. 'Positive thinking' has 'power', they think. Or they become stoic and even fatalistic about reality. Face the facts, they will say.

A recent illustration of this was the Christopher Reeve Super Bowl ad of a few years ago. Reeve, Hollywood's Superman, was tragically crippled by a horse-riding accident. But the ad showed him walking. Reeve consented to this ad because he believes that the greatest obstacle paralyzed people face is that they don't believe they'll walk again. 'The biggest problem, actually', he says, 'is people who've been in a chair for a very long time, because in order to survive psychologically they've had to accept "O.K., I'm going to spend my life in a chair."' Charles Krauthammer, a writer for *Time Magazine,* responded very critically to Reeve in an essay published on February 14, 2000. He complained that Reeve is undermining the very necessary step of facing reality. What is needed is not an unlikely-to-be-realized fantasy of a cure for those with severed spinal columns, but the determination to make a life for oneself from a wheelchair. 'They can have jobs and lives and careers', says Krauthammer. 'But they'll need to work very hard at it. And they'll need to start with precisely the psychological acceptance of reality that Reeve is so determined to undermine'.

This debate illustrates how the world struggles to find the balance. The Christian is in one sense more optimistic than Reeves, and more realistic than Krauthammer. Reality in this world is often hard. We are crippled emotionally, morally, spiritually, and even physically. We face and acknowledge this. We don't try to pretend it isn't so. 'In the world you will have tribulation', Jesus said. 'But,' He goes on to say, 'do not fear, for I have overcome the world' (John 16:33). We live in a wheelchair. We face tribulation. But Jesus has overcome it. His kingdom, power, and glory are forever. We will dwell in the house of the Lord forever.

This then shapes the outlook of our prayers and our entire lives. It gives us an essentially sunny disposition. We have a positive outlook. Whatever we endure in this life, life is short and eternity is long. Tim Keller (Sr Pastor at Redeemer PCA in New York) used the illustration of two people working the same job under the same awful conditions – eighty hours a week, terrible work environment, low pay, horrible people. One is promised a $100 bonus at the end of the year. The other is promised $15 million. Will the end reward color their experience in the present? Of course it will. For one, the job will be unbearable and endless. He will struggle all day, every day. For the other, the anticipation of his reward makes the hardship as if nothing. He can put up with anything, because it is temporary, and his reward will be great. Our view of the *future* profoundly effects our *present* state of mind. *Hope transforms despair into joy.* Jesus is able to 'endure the cross' because of 'joy set before Him' (Heb. 12:2). The cross was terrible. It had to be 'endured'. But knowledge of what lay ahead brought joy to him. Listen to the Apostle Paul:

> Therefore we do not lose heart, but though our outer man is decaying, yet our inner man is being renewed day by day. For momentary, light affliction is producing for us an eternal weight of glory far beyond all comparison, while we look not at the things which are seen, but at the things

which are not seen; for the things which are seen are temporal, but the things which are not seen are eternal (2 Cor. 4:16-18).

The 'outer man' he says, 'is decaying'. There is the realism. We break down, decay, and die. But this is mere 'momentary, light affliction' in light of the 'eternal weight of glory' that it produces. See how it transforms our view of current hardships? Momentary! Light! Again he says:

For I consider that the sufferings of this present time are not worthy to be compared with the glory that is to be revealed to us (Rom. 8:18).

Knowledge of 'the glory that is to be revealed' reduces today's trials to the level of things 'not worthy' of consideration. So incomparably greater is the glory that 'the suffering of this present time' can hardly be mentioned. *Hope transforms despair into joy!*

Praise

The concluding doxology is a plea and it is an expression of hope. But this is not all.

Third, the concluding doxology is an ascription of praise. It is, 'an expression of holy and joyful praise', says Pink (130). There is a sense in which this is a simple, yet exuberant concluding description of divine realities. We have turned to You in prayer and set these petitions before You because You are the King, You are the Almighty One, and You are all-glorious. Here is the reason why we pray to You. We began with praise. We end with praise. Why? Because You are worthy.

Because our hearts overflow with praise 'as we consider our needs, our dependence upon Him, our relation to Him', notes Lloyd-Jones, 'we must end as we begin, by praising Him'. Moreover, he says, 'The measure of our spirituality is the amount of praise and thanksgiving in our prayers' (77). Donald Coggan, the former Archbishop of Canterbury, summarizes where we've been in the Lord's Prayer and where we now are in these words:

> So the Prayer reaches its climax in words of adoration. It has taught us to think of God as *Father* ('Our Father'), as *King* ('Thy kingdom come'), as *Governor* ('Thy will be done'), as *Provider* ('Give us ... bread'), as *Deliverer* ('Deliver us from evil'). The prayer, which began with the adoration of God and proceeded to petition swings back to the God-centered attitude of adoration in the Doxology – 'Thine is the kingdom, and the power, and the glory, for ever' (40).

Does your heart overflow with praise? Is it your great passion that God should be worshiped and honored? This is a 'measure' of our commitment to Christ and our surrender to His will. We are focused on His honor. We are content when He is honored. We want nothing more than we want His glory.

This is how we pray and live. We are citizens of God's kingdom, and it is 'forever'. His power will protect us forever. His glory will be manifest forever. In the meantime, we keep watching and praying, anticipating the glorious day when the already meets the not yet. Amen? Yes indeed, truly, may it be so!

V

Persistence

13

Ask, Seek, Knock

Ask, and it shall be given to you; seek, and you shall find; knock, and it shall be opened to you. For everyone who asks receives, and he who seeks finds, and to him who knocks it shall be opened. Or what man is there among you, when his son shall ask him for a loaf, will give him a stone? Or if he shall ask for a fish, he will not give him a snake, will he? If you then, being evil, know how to give good gifts to your children, how much more shall your Father who is in heaven give what is good to those who ask Him! (Matt. 7:7-11).

Further along in the Sermon on the Mount (the body of teaching in which the Lord's Prayer is found) Jesus provides an additional lesson on prayer, specifically on *persistence* in prayer (7:7-11). We include this in a study on the Lord's Prayer because of our understanding of its role within the whole Sermon on the Mount. The connection between 7:7-11 and all that preceded it in Matthew 5:3–7:6 is that of prayer's vital role in enabling the disciples of Christ to fulfill the requirements of discipleship as found in the Sermon on the Mount. Prayer, modeled on the Lord's Prayer, is the means by which we are conformed to the ideals of Christ for His disciples. For example, Jesus said that we were to be *discerning*, not casting our pearls before swine (7:6). Yet He also said that we were not to judge (7:1-5). How then are we to make that razor's edge distinction between judging (which is forbidden) and discerning (which is required)? This is a difficult thing. We need help. We are not able to do this on our own. We need the grace of God. We need the illumination of the Holy Spirit. How are we to get it? We must pray, particularly prayers modeled on the Lord's Prayer. What is true of judging and discerning is also true of all that Jesus has said in the Sermon on the Mount about the Christian life. Let us elaborate.

Prayer as a Means

How are we to trust God and not be anxious about our lives, about what we shall eat, or drink, or wear? Will we ever be able to live in the confidence of God's supply and provision? We will do so only as we pray after the manner of Jesus' instruction.

How are we to seek first the kingdom and His righteousness (Matt. 6:25-34)? How are we to become heavenly minded, content with what we have, laying up treasures in heaven rather than upon earth? How are we to resist the idolatry of attempting to serve God and mammon (Matt. 6:19-24)? Not in our own strength. Not by our own wisdom and power. This is possible only through prayer.

How are we to avoid the hypocrisy of 'practicing (our) righteousness before men to be noticed by them' of sounding the trumpet before we give, of standing on street corners when we pray, and of putting on gloomy faces when we fast (Matt. 6:1-18)? Will our righteousness ever exceed the superficial and external righteousness of the scribes and the Pharisees? Will we not only avoid murder, but the hatred that leads to the murder? Will we not only avoid adultery, but the lust that leads to adultery? Will we ever take sin so seriously so as to cut off the offending hand and pluck out the offending eye? Will we ever become a people whose 'yes is yes' and whose 'no is no'; who turn the other cheek; who give the coats off our backs; who walk the extra mile; who love not only our neighbors but also our enemies, thereby demonstrating that we are children of our Father who is in heaven? Are we ever to be perfect as our Father in heaven is perfect? (Matt. 5:17-48).

How desperate we are for help! How weak we are and how hopeless it all is! How will we ever become the 'salt of the earth', 'the light of the world', and a 'city set upon a hill' (Matt. 5:13-16)? Will others ever see our good works and so glorify our Father who is in heaven? What about the Beatitudes? Will we ever be 'poor in spirit'? Will we ever 'mourn' for our sins? Will we ever be meek? Will we ever 'hunger and thirst after righteousness'? Will we be merciful? Will we be 'pure in heart'? Will we be 'peacemakers'? Will we rejoice in persecutions? (Matt. 5:12-13). The answer implied by verses 7:1-11 is that we will become disciples of this sort only by prayer. We need the grace of God, the help of God, the power of God, the wisdom of God, and the Spirit of God. How do I access that help, grace and power? By asking. This is the natural connection between verses 7:7-11 and all that has preceded them. Jesus is presenting prayer as the means by which we will be able to become all that Jesus commands us to be in the Sermon on the Mount. Jesus is saying, 'Ask and it (godliness) shall be given to you, seek and you shall find (spiritual maturity), knock and it (Christ-likeness) shall be opened to you'. Jesus 'assures them that such gifts are theirs if sought through prayer', says Carson (186). Jesus speaks of prayer, says Matthew Henry, 'as the appointed means of attaining what we need, especially grace to obey the precepts He had given'.

The parallel in Luke clarifies this point:

> If you then, being evil, know how to give good gifts to your children, how much more shall your heavenly Father give the Holy Spirit to those who ask Him? (Luke 11:13).

What is termed 'good things' in Matthew 7:11 is defined more narrowly in Luke as the 'Holy Spirit'. This clarifies Jesus' intent and primary application. The Father will give His Spirit to those who ask. By the Spirit we will become all that Jesus outlines in the Sermon on the Mount. By the Spirit we will be given the help, and the grace, and the power to be the disciples of Christ.

It is absolutely essential that we grasp this point. Often we become frustrated by the demands of Christian discipleship. We find ourselves falling into the same mistakes over and over. How will we ever break out of our shallow molds? How will we ever progress in sanctification, become Christlike, be characterized by the Beatitudes, or manifest the fruit of the Holy Spirit (Gal. 5:19ff)? It can seem overwhelming to us. I despair of ever becoming the person that God wants me to be. The answer that Jesus gives is this – you can by prayer. You must *ask* for it.

You must *seek* it. You must *knock* down the door of
grace. Then you will *receive* and *find* and it will be
opened to you. Do you want to become a true man or
woman of God? This, then, is the key. Having already
taught us how to pray (Matt. 6:5-15), Jesus now teaches
us about persistence, efficacy, and confidence in prayer.

Persistence in Prayer

> Ask, and it shall be given to you; seek, and you
> shall find; knock, and it shall be opened to you
> (Matt. 7:7).

The three verbs in verse 7, 'ask', 'seek', 'knock', are all
present imperatives. The present tense indicates
'continuous action' says Morris (170). Jesus is
commending 'continuous, persistent prayer' adds
France (177). His point is that *effective* prayer is
persistent prayer. The sense of the verse is, 'keep on
asking and it will be given to you, keep on seeking and
you will find, keep on knocking and it will be opened
to you'. Jesus ties together persistence and efficacy.
Prayer works as you work at prayer.

We shouldn't look for much distinction between
the meaning of these verbs. There are nuances of
meaning, but basically they are three ways of saying
the same thing. What are we doing in prayer? We are
asking, we are seeking, we are knocking. It is likely to
be the case that the latter two terms should be
understood somewhat more broadly. We 'ask' in
prayer. We 'seek' God and His grace in prayer. But we
also seek God in His word and among His people.
Similarly *knocking* may have in mind all the means of
grace, including prayer but beyond prayer. We are to

persist in asking for, seeking after, and knocking down doors in pursuit of God's help, grace, and power.

Persistence, however, should not be seen as an end in itself, but rather as an indication of earnestness and sincerity. Jesus is not commanding mechanical persistence, for He has already warned us against 'meaningless repetition' (Matt. 6:7). It is not words for words' sake that he commands us to persist in. Rather, persistence is commended as an indication that 1) we believe, and 2) that we are earnest or sincere. I persist in prayer because I believe that prayer makes a difference, because I believe that God responds to the prayers of His people. I persist also because I am sincere and earnest. A man courting a woman persists in pursuing her. If he seeks her hand in marriage he is not put off by her initial indifference. He persists. By doing so he does not earn her affection, but he does demonstrate his sincerity and earnestness. His is not a temporary or a marginal desire. He wants her with all of his heart. An athlete pursuing a gold medal at the Olympics persists in training. His discipline does not earn him a medal. But if he were to slack off it would demonstrate insincerity, that he doesn't *really* want the medal. In each case persistence is an indication of sincerity, earnestness and conviction. If either one quits it indicates that he is no longer earnest or convinced of the goal.

Sincerity is critical in prayer even as insincerity dooms prayer to failure. Persistence is commended because it proves the earnestness of the desire. We demonstrate sincerity by going to God in prayer and persisting there. The depth and integrity of our desire is proven by returning to Him again and again, persistently asking and requesting that He might hear and respond. If we look again at the parallel passage in Luke we see clearly that this is the point. Jesus told the following parable:

> And He said to them, 'Suppose one of you shall have a friend, and shall go to him at midnight, and say to him, "Friend, lend me three loaves; for a friend of mine has come to me from a journey, and I have nothing to set before him"; and from inside he shall answer and say, "Do not bother me; the door has already been shut and my children and I are in bed; I cannot get up and give you anything." I tell you, even though he will not get up and give him anything because he is his friend, yet because of his persistence he will get up and give him as much as he needs' (Luke 11:5-8).

Then His point of application was:

> And I say to you, ask, and it shall be given to you; seek, and you shall find; knock, and it shall be opened to you (Luke 11:9).

The point of the parable is that 'because of his persistence' the man shall get what he needs from his friend. The application of the parable to prayer is 'ask and it shall be given to you, seek and you shall find, knock and it shall be opened to you'. Persistence demonstrates the urgency or importance of the matter. Jesus taught the same thing yet again:

> Now He was telling them a parable to show that at all times they ought to pray and not to lose heart, 'There was in a certain city a judge who did not fear God, and did not respect man. And there was

a widow in that city, and she kept coming to him, saying, "Give me legal protection from my opponent." And for a while he was unwilling; but afterward he said to himself, "Even though I do not fear God nor respect man, yet because this widow bothers me, I will give her legal protection, lest by continually coming she wear me out.'" And the Lord said, 'Hear what the unrighteous judge said; now shall not God bring about justice for His elect, who cry to Him day and night, and will He delay long over them' (Luke 18:1-7).

The point of the parable? That 'at all times they ought to pray and not to lose heart'. In other words, the point is persistence. Even an unjust judge responds to persistent requests. How much more will a good God.

I fear that one of the reasons we lack spiritual depth in our day is because of our failure to persist in prayer. Where do we lack it? We lack it in our family life. Our families are not as strong and as spiritually stable as they ought to be. We lack it in our personal lives. We are not progressing in sanctification as we ought. We lack it as a church. We are not seeing revival to any significant degree in our day. We are failing to reach our neighbors and our neighborhoods. Why are these things so? Because we don't pray, and, when we do pray, we trifle at it. We are not patient in prayer. We are not persistent in prayer. We may spend a few minutes in prayer, pray a few lines, and then we move on to the next thing. We are not continually asking, and seeking, and knocking. Consequently, we are demonstrating to God either that we don't believe that prayer really changes things, or that these things are not critical to us. We lack faith. Our prayers lack earnestness and sincerity because they lack confidence.

We are not sure that prayer works. We are not sure that it makes any difference. We are not sure that there is any power in it. So we fire off a quick request and move on. This is not the prayer that Jesus commands or commends, and it is not the prayer that works. Answers require persistence!

Efficacy in Prayer
Now we may look more closely at Jesus' promise of the efficacy of prayer.

> For everyone who asks receives, and he who seeks finds, and to him who knocks it shall be opened (Matt. 7:8).

Jesus repeats the promises a second time. Indeed within two sentences He promises six times that He will answer our prayers. He says again that when we ask we will receive, when we seek we will find, when we knock it will be opened to us. His point is that prayer is 'efficacious', says Morris. It 'gets things done' (169, 170). There is a direct connection between asking and receiving, between seeking and finding, and between knocking and it being opened. This is true not just for a spiritual elite, or for important people, or for church leaders. He says for '*everyone*' who 'asks', and 'seeks', and 'knocks', they shall 'receive' and 'find' and it shall be 'opened'. There are none who are too insignificant, or too lowly, or too immature. Jesus speaks of a God who is ready and willing to hear our prayers and grant our requests. He does not have to be bullied or cajoled into answering our prayers.

As we have seen before, there is hardly anything in all the world for us that is more difficult to believe than the fact that prayer makes a difference. We believe that our witness makes a difference. We believe that our teaching and preaching make an important impact for good. We believe that Christian living in the home provides an important model. We believe that Christian witness in the world builds the kingdom of Christ. Still, it is difficult for us to believe that prayer makes any positive contribution. We live in a materialistic age, an age in which all that is real is that which we can see, handle, taste, and touch. Reality is the material reality. It is difficult for us to acknowledge any reality beyond that which is physical. Yet the Bible says the things that we see are temporal and the unseen things are eternal (2 Cor. 4:18). The Bible teaches that we are to walk by faith and not by sight (2 Cor. 5:7). On the authority of Jesus Himself we are promised that there is a direct relationship between asking and receiving, between seeking and finding, and between knocking and the door being opened to us. We can put it negatively to make the point as well. There is a relationship between not asking and not receiving, not seeking and not finding, not knocking and the door not being opened to us. If we do not ask, seek and knock we will not receive, find, or have it opened to us. James warns us plainly: 'we have not because we ask not' (Jas. 4:2).

There is a direct connection between faithfulness in prayer and God granting to us those things which we need. Scripture abounds in examples. When Moses lifts up his hands in prayer the children of Israel prevail in battle against the Amalekites. When he begins to tire and his arms droop and his prayers slacken, they begin to fail (Exod. 17:8-13). As Daniel began to pray for the release of Israel from captivity, from that moment God began to act. The angel Gabriel says to Daniel:

> At the beginning of your supplications the command was issued, and I have come to tell you, for you are highly esteemed (Dan. 9:23a).

Again he is told:

> Do not be afraid, Daniel, for from the first day that you set your heart on understanding this and on humbling yourself before your God, your words were heard, and I have come in response to your words (Dan. 10:12).

The direct connection between asking and receiving could hardly be made more explicit. 'At the beginning of your supplication the command was given'. Again, 'from the first day ... your words were heard, *and I have come in response to your words*'.

This efficacy is assumed throughout the New Testament. Paul urges the Romans:

> Now I urge you, brethren, by our Lord Jesus Christ and by the love of the Spirit, to strive together with me in your prayers to God for me, that I may be delivered from those who are disobedient in Judea, and that my service for Jerusalem may prove acceptable to the saints; so that I may come to you in joy by the will of God and find refreshing rest in your company (Rom. 15:30-32).

Why pray? 'That I may be delivered', he says, 'so that I may come to you'. Through prayer Paul may be saved from his enemies, and be able to continue his ministry among them.

Paul tells the Corinthians that God will deliver him from his enemies. He says:

> And He will yet deliver us, you also joining in helping us through your prayers, that thanks may be given by many persons on our behalf for the favor bestowed upon us through the prayers of many (2 Cor. 1:10b-11).

Their prayers help. By prayer they are actually 'joining in helping' him. He says 'favor' was 'bestowed' on him 'through the prayers of many'. Prayer is efficacious.

He writes to the Ephesians:

> With all prayer and petition pray at all times in the Spirit, and with this in view, be on the alert with all perseverance and petition for all the saints, and pray on my behalf, that utterance may be given to me in the opening of my mouth, to make known with boldness the mystery of the gospel, for which I am an ambassador in chains; that in proclaiming it I may speak boldly, as I ought to speak (Eph. 6:18-20).

He commands persistence ('pray at all times ... with all perseverance and petition') with the result that greater facility and boldness in speech will be given to him. 'Pray', he says, 'that utterance may be given to me' and 'that I may speak boldly'. Prayer is not an empty religious exercise but the means by which these capacities and opportunities will actually be given.

He writes to the Philippians:

> For I know that this shall turn out for my deliverance through your prayers and the provision of the Spirit of Jesus Christ (Phil. 1:19).

How will he be delivered from prison? 'Through your prayers', he says, the Spirit of Christ will make 'provision'.

He writes to the Colossians:

Devote yourselves to prayer, keeping alert in it with an attitude of thanksgiving; praying at the same time for us as well, that God may open up to us a door for the word, so that we may speak forth the mystery of Christ, for which I have also been imprisoned; in order that I may make it clear in the way I ought to speak (Col. 4:2-4).

He asks them to pray for a 'door for the word' to open because he believes that prayer is the means through which such a door will indeed open. The Apostles everywhere assume and are convinced that there is a unique efficacy in prayer. Prayer opens doors. Prayer gives facility in speech. Prayer works. Prayer makes a difference. God responds to our prayers.

Confidence in Prayer

Now Jesus explains *why* prayer 'works'. It is effective because the God to whom we pray is our Father.

Or what man is there among you, when his son shall ask him for a loaf, will give him a stone? Or if he shall ask for a fish, he will not give him a snake, will he? If you then, being evil, know how to give good gifts to your children, how much more shall your Father who is in heaven give what is good to those who ask Him! (Matt. 7:9-11).

Jesus provides us with the example of fathers with their sons. When a son comes and asks his father for a loaf, he doesn't mock him by giving him a stone, does he? The commentators suggest that Jesus may have particularly in mind a stone of that region that looks like a loaf of bread. Again, if a son asks his father for a fish, he will not give him a snake, will he? Several of the commentators point out that the catfish in the sea of Galilee looked very eel-like, and could be mistaken for a snake. Jesus' point then would be that a good father doesn't trick his son by giving him a snake when he is asking him for a fish. This is true of virtually all fathers. Even though we are 'evil', we do give good gifts to our children. This is almost universally the case. Notice that Jesus assumes the depravity of man. 'If you then, being evil, know how to give good gifts to your children'. Morris notes that Jesus 'assumes this as so basic that it can be taken for granted ... the solidarity of the race in sin is taken as a basic fact' (171). The argument, then, is one from the lesser to the greater. If evil fathers are good to their children and give good gifts to them, then how much more can we, who are children of our perfectly righteous Father in heaven, depend upon Him to give those things that are good for us? If we persist in prayer, trusting in His goodness, we can pray confidently knowing that God will give to us the good things that we seek.

There may be times that we're not seeking 'what is good'. There may be occasions on which we are asking for things that are unwise or contrary to the will of God. The promise is not to give us whatever we might ask for without any restrictions whatsoever. No good father would give to his child everything that he asks. Sometimes we ask foolishly, sometimes we ask sinfully. We return again to what James says:

You ask and do not receive, because you ask with wrong motives, so that you may spend it on your pleasures (Jas. 4:3).

As we saw in chapter 2, sometimes our motives are warped and distorted and sinful. The Rev. J. A. Motyer used to warn his students that if God didn't say 'no' to our prayers, prayer would be the equivalent of a loaded gun pointed at our heads. We would ask foolishly and unwisely. And if God were obligated to answer us we would quickly bring destructive forces to play in our lives. We would stop praying immediately. We could not bear the responsibility. One of God's graces to us is that He says 'no' when we ask for things that will not be beneficial or edifying for us. What He gives is 'what is good', or 'good gifts'. This is consistent with what is said elsewhere about praying 'according to His will' (1 John 5:14, 15). Your Father will give to you the *good* things you seek from His hand.

The question is: What do you want? Are you seeking 'good gifts', as God defines good? Are you seeking to become a man or woman of God? Do you want to be poor in spirit, meek and merciful? Do you want to be pure in heart, and hunger and thirst after righteousness? Do you want to be the salt of the earth, the light of the world, and a city set out on a hill? Do you want your righteousness to exceed that of the scribes and the Pharisees? Do you want to be perfect, as your Father in heaven is perfect? Do you want to practice your righteousness in secret, and not before men as the hypocrites do? Do you want to lay up your treasures in heaven and not on earth? Do you want to serve God alone and not God and mammon? Do you want to trust God and not be anxious about life and about what you shall eat or drink, or with what you will clothe yourself? Do you want to seek first the kingdom and its righteousness? Do you want avoid judgmentalism and yet to be discerning?

Then you will need to pray. And if this is what you really want you are going to persist in your prayer. You are going to plead. You are going to beg. You are going to return again and again, asking, beseeching, seeking, knocking, until you get that which you require. And you can pray in the confidence that your Father will hear that prayer. The question is, What do you want?

Second, do you *really* want it? Do you *really* want to be a man or woman of God? If you do, then persistence will come naturally. You won't have to be brow-beaten by the preacher into praying. You won't have to be scolded and exhorted to pray. You will pray. You will pray in the confidence that your Father is going to give you the 'good things' you seek, and persist because these are the things that are crucial to you and to Him. These are the things – holiness, godliness, purity, integrity, fruitfulness – that are important above all, the things that are truly vital and foremost upon your heart and His. You'll be pleading for the souls of your children. You'll be pleading for your own soul. You'll be pleading for the souls of your neighbors around you. And God will be granting your request.

George Müller of Bristol prayed for over sixty-three years for the conversion of a friend. 'Never give up until the answer comes', he said. 'He is not converted yet', he noted, 'but he will be' (*The Kneeling Christian*, 95). This is persistence and confidence in prayer!

The only thing standing between us and personal godliness, sanctified homes, and revival in our church and community is persistent and efficacious prayer. Don't think for a moment that the people in the Bible, whose prayers were gloriously answered, were any different from us. James not only says that 'you have not because you ask not', but he also says, 'the effective prayer of a righteous man can accomplish much' (Jas. 5:16). He then says:

Elijah was a man with a nature like ours, and he prayed earnestly that it might not rain; and it did not rain on the earth for three years and six months. And he prayed again, and the sky poured rain, and the earth produced its fruit (Jas. 5:17, 18).

Elijah was a man 'with a nature like ours'. In other words, he was just like one of us. Yet he prayed earnestly that it might not rain, and it didn't rain. Then he prayed again for rain and it rained. James' point is that Elijah is the same as we are, a man of 'like passions' (KJV). We are sinners saved by grace standing in the same relationship with God. We too can offer prayers that are 'effective' and 'accomplish much'. Jesus promises that our persistent prayers, prayers that are earnest and sincere, will be heard by our Father, and that He will grant our requests. Let us then get about the business of praying following the model Jesus has provided in the Lord's Prayer and persisting as He has just urged. Let us begin to ask and seek and knock. Let us trifle with prayer no longer. Let us pray 'night and day' (1 Thess. 3:10). Let us 'pray without ceasing' (1 Thess. 5:17). Let us 'devote' ourselves to prayer (Col. 4:2). Let us 'pray at all times' with 'all prayer' (Eph. 6:18). Let us 'always' pray, as Jesus said, and 'not lose heart' (Luke 18:1). Let us then see the bounty of God poured out among us.

14

The Lessons of the Lord's Prayer

It remains for us now to recap and reinforce what we have learned about prayer from the model prayer that Jesus has provided. Jesus is answering a fundamental question, a question to which we all want answers, and with which we have all wrestled. How am I to relate to God? How am I to communicate with Him? How am I to address Him? There is no more fundamental question than this. It is possible that because these studies have been spread out over many pages the main points have been lost in the details. Consequently, we will review the primary lessons that Jesus teaches in order that we might better apply them to our own lives.

Pray
First, Jesus teaches us to pray. This may seem an obvious point, but I make it anyway. There are disciplines or practices that nourish our spiritual lives. Jesus mentions three that were common in His day: giving, fasting, and prayer. He says, 'when you pray' (Matt. 6:5-7, 9). He expects that we will pray. He tells us that there are things that we should not do in prayer: we should not stand on street corners 'in order to be seen by men',

but rather 'pray to your Father who is in secret' (Matt. 6:6). And we should not babble on endlessly with meaningless repetitions, as though length of time in prayer or the number of words uttered were in any sense meritorious or keys to earning the desired response from God (6:7, 8). But do pray. Why? Because this is how we honor and praise God. Because this is how we receive what only God can give. Because prayer changes us and changes things. Because prayer makes a difference. When we ask we receive, when we seek we find; when we knock it is opened (Matt. 7:7, 8).

Our Father

Second, Jesus teaches us to pray to our Father in heaven. How are we to address the One to whom we pray? 'Our Father'. Because of what Christ has done, our sins are forgiven and we are adopted into the family of God. This is not a right of birth but of rebirth. John writes:

> But as many as received Him, to them He gave the right to become children of God, even to those who believe in His name, who were born not of blood, nor of the will of the flesh, nor of the will of man, but of God (John 1:12, 13).

Adoption, or sonship, is a 'right' given to those who 'believe' and are 'born ... of God'. I pray then as a child to a Father. I pray with all the confidence and security of a child in the lap of his father. We are pitied 'as a father pities his children' (Ps. 103:13). He is our Father 'in heaven'. So we always approach our Father with reverence and godly fear. Yet we are confident that He listens to us with pleasure and favor. He knows how to give good gifts to His children when they ask (Matt. 7:11). If we ask for a fish He will not give us a snake. If we ask for bread He will not give us a stone (Matt. 7:9, 10). We bow our heads in prayer confident and secure in our relationship to our Father, certain of His love and care (Matt. 6:25-34).

God-Centered

Third, Jesus teaches us to place God in the center of our prayers. We are tempted to take a 'shopping list' approach to prayer, to begin and end with ourselves, with our needs and desires and plans, with give me this, and this, and this. But this is not the pattern taught by Jesus. His prayer begins with the praise of God. God is identified (and by implication honored) as a Father who is in heaven, that is, as One who rules and reigns over all from His throne in heaven. The first three petitions are all concerned with God's agenda – His name, kingdom, and will. As we have seen, we ask for His name to be hallowed, His kingdom to come, and His will to be done on earth as it is in heaven *even before we ask for bread!* In our prayers and hearts God and His concerns come even before the most basic and essential human needs. His name, kingdom and will come before even our own physical survival! We have repeatedly made the point that we pray in this way not merely because there is a form into which we rigidly pour our prayers, but because this is what flows from our hearts. We are hungering and thirsting after righteousness. We are seeking first His kingdom. Like Jesus, we have food to eat which the world does not know about. Our food is to do the will of our Father (John 4:32-34). Because His name, kingdom, and will are first on our hearts, because they are our passion and primary concern, they are first on our lips in prayer. We pray as we live, and we live as we pray.

Then when we begin to reason with God as to why He ought to hear our prayers, when we begin to plead, we do so primarily in terms of what honors and pleases Him. Answer our prayers, we plead, because Yours is the kingdom, the power, and the glory. It is in your interest to do so. You will be glorified if You do so. Your kingdom will grow and advance if You do so. We are learning in prayer to want what God wants for the reasons God wants it. Do you see how thoroughly God-centered this prayer is? Even when we do pray for ourselves, at least two of three petitions (forgiveness and deliverance from evil) have to do with victory over sin or with living a holy and God-pleasing life. Jesus is teaching us that God is to be at the center of our prayers. Our prayers are not to be taken up wholly with physical and material needs and concerns. They have a place, but they should never be primary. Our prayers should not be predominantly about health and vocational issues, as is typically the case with prayer lists and prayer meetings. They should primarily be about the things of God and matters of the Spirit. The condition of our souls, our sanctification, the salvation of the lost, the progress of the kingdom of God, are all the main matters for our prayers.

Dependence

Fourth, Jesus teaches us to pray with an awareness of our absolute dependence upon God. Is this not this the point of praying for bread and deliverance from evil? Is this not the implication of admitting that we are weak and needful? By praying for help are we not admitting our own inadequacy? This is surely the case. If we are to

resist temptation and evil we will need the grace of
God. Left to ourselves we will fail and fall. We have
no ability to lead holy lives, to love our neighbor, to
please God and serve God. Apart from Christ we can
do nothing (John 15:5). This fact is made all the more
certain by the petition for bread. We might have
thought that this was one thing that we could do. I
may not be able to be good but I can make money! I
know how to work! No, the power to make wealth is
God-given. Remember God's warning to Israel not to
forget that He is the source of their wealth:

> Otherwise, you may say in your heart, 'My power
> and the strength of my hand made me this wealth'.
> But you shall remember the Lord your God, for it
> is He who is giving you power to make wealth,
> that He may confirm His covenant which He
> swore to your fathers, as it is this day (Deut 8:17,
> 18).

Good health, a good mind, good opportunities, and all
other assets are God's gifts. I cannot do anything –
generate wealth, be a good spouse, be a good parent,
be a good employee or employer, be a contributing
member of the church, lead a God-pleasing life –
nothing – I can't do anything apart from Christ. I am
absolutely dependent upon Him for all good, for
everything.

An awareness of this weakness is the key to our true
strength because it drives us to prayer (2 Cor. 12:7-10).
The times in my life when I have been most devoted
to prayer have been those in which I was most keenly
aware of my weakness. I was certain in college that I
could not resist evil without the power of the Holy

Spirit, and so I sought it in prayer daily for extended periods of time. Perhaps there have been times for you when you encountered a heart that was stubbornly resistant to change, and became aware that only God could change it. You gained a glimpse of your state of absolute dependence upon God. We can plant and water, but only God can cause growth (1 Cor. 3:6). If I am to do anything, accomplish anything, contribute anything, amount to anything, it will only be by the blessing of God, to which we have access by prayer.

Pleading

Fifth, Jesus teaches us to plead in prayer. Too often we toy at prayer. We rattle off a list of things we want. We 'say' our prayers. We state a few generalized petitions – 'God bless Jimmy and Suzie. God bless the church. God bless the whole world.' But there is little indication that we truly want it, or have thought it through, or know why our Father ought to give it. Hallow Your name, give us bread, and keep us from evil, Jesus prays. Why? He gives reasons. 'For' or 'because' Yours is 'the kingdom, the power and glory'. You have an *interest* in granting these petitions and You have the *ability*. In this fashion, Jesus reasons with His Father. God is not a machine to which we present lists. He is not a tape recorder or a celestial answering machine. He is a Person, and we are to make our case to Him even as we would to our earthly fathers or to a judge in his court. So we plead, and argue, and persuade even with importunity. Passion in prayer is entirely appropriate. 'O God, give me Scotland or I die', cried the Reformer, John Knox. 'Blot me out from Thy book', said Moses, if you will not forgive your people (Exod. 32:32). Provide me with a job, change my child's heart, save my neighbor, because these are things that will be best for them, bring You honor, glorify Your name, build Your kingdom, exalt Christ, defeat evil, and humble the devil. Plead and beg and argue and make your case to a God who is your Father and who invites you to reason with Him. Let me say from personal experience that this kind of praying will change your prayer life. How? God will seem more alive and real to you. Your prayers will come alive, and so will the One to whom you are addressing your concerns.

Persistence

Sixth, Jesus teaches us to persist in prayer. 'Keep on asking, keep on seeking, keep on knocking', Jesus said (Matt. 7:7). Those who persist in prayer, who pray 'always' and do not 'lose heart' are promised that they will receive, find, and that doors will open for them. Persistence is valued not as mechanical or 'meaningless repetition', but as a sign of our earnestness or sincerity. We are not to trifle at prayer. Our prayers are to be grounded in the conviction that God hears our prayers and that they are efficacious. Because they are, we are urgent and persistent. Pray 'all day and all night', Isaiah told the watchmen of Israel, 'and give Him no rest until He establishes and makes Jerusalem a praise in the earth' (Isa. 62:7).

Forever

Finally, Jesus teaches us to pray with eternity in view. 'Forever,' He says. We pray what we pray and request what we request because God's kingdom, power, and glory are forever. This is the perspective from which we live and pray. In recent days I've come to the conviction that there has been too much of this world in my ministry, and too little of eternity. Jesus constantly motivates us by appealing to the rewards of heaven or the curses of hell. This is repeatedly the case in the Sermon on the Mount (5:3, 8, 10, 12, 19, 22, 25, 29, 30; 6:1, 4, 6, 18). Why do we pray God-centered and kingdom-centered prayers? Because we've learned to sit loose to this world. Because 'the world is passing away and also its lusts; but the one who does the will of God abides forever' (1 John 2:17). Because life is short and eternity is long. Because it doesn't profit a man to gain the whole world and lose his own soul (Matt. 16:26). Because where your treasure is, there will your heart be also (Matt. 6:21).

These are a few of the lessons of the Lord's Prayer. Prayer is to have an important place in our lives. We pray to our sympathetic Father, God-centered and kingdom-centered prayers, with dependent hearts, with urgency and pleadings, with the eternal perspective in view. Such prayers the Father is pleased to receive.

VI

Appendix, Bibliography, Index

Appendix

A Paraphrase on the Lord's Prayer, in
Scripture Expressions – **Matthew Henry**[1]

Matthew Henry concluded his *A Method for Prayer* with chapters in which he included a paraphrase of the Lord's Prayer and 'some short forms of prayer' to help those who had difficulty composing prayers for themselves. As he 'dialates' (*sic*) or elaborates upon each line, Henry provides a wealth of devotional Scriptural expression to help us to pray as Jesus taught His disciples to pray.

* * *

The Lord's prayer being intended not only for a form of prayer itself, but a rule of direction, a plan or model in little, by which we may frame our prayers; and the expressions being remarkably concise and yet vastly comprehensive, it will be of good use sometimes to lay it before us, and observing the method and order of it, to dilate upon the several passages and petitions of it, that we may use it the more intelligently; of which we shall only here give a specimen, in the assistance we may have from some other scriptures.

---

[1]Henry, Matthew *A Method for Prayer* (ed. Duncan), 190-207.

1. Our Father which art in heaven.

O Lord our God, doubtless thou art our Father, though Abraham be ignorant of us, and Israel acknowledge us not; thou, O Lord, art our Father, our Redeemer, thy name is from everlasting (Isa. 63:16); and we will from this time cry unto thee, our Father, thou art the guide of our youth (Jer. 3:4).

Have we not all one Father? Has not one God created us? (Mal. 2:10). Thou art the Father of our spirits, to whom we ought to be in subjection and live (Heb. 12:9).

Thou art the Father of lights (Jas. 1:17), and the Father of mercies, and the God of all consolation (2 Cor. 1:3): The eternal Father (Isa. 9:6), of whom, and through whom, and to whom, are all things (Rom. 11:36).

Thou art the Father of our Lord Jesus Christ (Eph. 1:3), whose glory was that of the only begotten of the Father, who is in his bosom (John 1:14, 18), by him, as one brought up with him, daily his delight, and rejoicing always before him (Prov. 8:30).

Thou art in Christ, our Father, and the Father of all believers, whom thou has predestinated to the adoption of children (Eph. 1:5), and into whose hearts thou hast sent the Spirit of the Son, teaching them to cry Abba, Father (Gal. 4:6), behold what manner of love the Father hath bestowed upon us, that we should be called the children of God (1 John 3:1). That the Lord God Almighty should be to us a Father, and we should be to him for sons and daughters (2 Cor. 6:18): And that as many as receive Christ, to them thou shouldest give power to become the sons of God, even to them that believe on his name; which are born, not of the will of man, but of God, and his grace (John 1:12, 13).

O that we may receive the adoption of sons (Gal. 4:5), and that as obedient and genuine children we may fashion ourselves according to the example of him who hath called us, who is holy (1 Pet. 1:14, 15); and may be followers of God as dear children (Eph. 5:1), and conformed to the image of his Son, who is the first-born among many brethren (Rom. 8:29).

Enable us to come to thee with humble boldness and confidence (Eph. 3:12), as to a Father, a tender Father, who spares us as a man spares his son who serves him (Mal. 3:17); and as having an advocate with the Father (1 John 2:1), who yet has told us, that the Father himself loves us (John 16:27).

Thou art a Father, but where is thine honour (Mal. 1:6)? Lord, give us grace to serve thee as becomes children, with reverence and godly fear (Heb. 12:28).

Thou art a Father, and if earthly parents, being evil, yet know how to give good gifts to their children, how much more shall our heavenly Father, give the Holy Spirit to them that ask him (Luke 11:13). Lord, give us the spirit of grace and supplication (Zech. 12:10).

We come to thee as prodigal children, that have gone from our Father's house into a far country; but we will arise and go to our Father, for in his house there is bread enough, and to spare; and if we continue at a distance from him, we perish with hunger. Father, we have sinned against heaven, and before thee, and are no more worthy to be called thy children, make us even as thy hired servants (Luke 15:13, 17-19).

Thou art our Father in heaven and therefore unto thee, O Lord, do we lift our souls (Ps. 86:4, 16). Unto thee we lift up our eyes, O thou that dwellest in the heavens: As the eyes of a servant are to the hand of his master and the eyes of a maiden to the hand of her mistress, so do our eyes wait upon thee, O Lord our God (Ps. 123:1-2); a God whom the heaven of heavens cannot contain, and yet whom we may have access to (1 Kgs. 8:27), having a High-Priest that is passed into the heavens as our forerunner (Heb. 4:14).

Thou, O God, dwellest in the high and holy place (Isa. 57:15), and holy and reverend is his name (Ps. 111:9). God is in heaven, and we are upon the earth (Eccles. 5:2), therefore should we choose our words to reason with him (Job 9:14), and yet through a Mediator we have boldness to enter into the holiest (Heb. 10:19).

Look down, we pray thee, from heaven, and behold, from the habitation of thy holiness, and of thy glory (Isa. 63:15), and have compassion upon us, and help us (Mark 9:22). Heaven is the firmament of thy power (Ps. 150:1): O hear us from thy holy heaven, with the saving strength of thy right hand; send us help from thy sanctuary, and strengthen us out of Zion (Ps. 20:2, 6).

And, O that, since heaven is our Father's house (John 14:2), we may have our conversation there (Phil. 3:20), and may seek things that are above (Col. 3:1).

2. *Hallowed be thy Name.*

And now, what is our petition, and what is our request (Esther 5:6)? What would we that thou shouldest do for us (Matt. 20:32)? This is our heart's desire and prayer in the first place (Rom. 10:1), Father, in heaven, let thy name be sanctified. We pray that thou mayest be glorified as a holy God (Lev. 10:3).

We desire to exalt the Lord our God, to worship at his footstool, at his holy hill, and to praise his great and terrible name, for it is holy, for the Lord our God is holy (Lev. 10:3). Thou art holy, O thou that inhabitest the praises of Israel (Ps. 22:3).

We glory in thy holy name, and therefore shall our hearts rejoice (Ps. 105:3), because that we have trusted in that holy name of thine (Ps. 33:21), to which we will always give thanks, and triumph in thy praise (Ps. 106:47).

Lord enable us to glorify thy holy name forevermore, by praising thee with all our hearts (Ps. 86:12), and by bringing forth much fruit, for herein is our heavenly Father glorified (John 15:8). O that we may be to our God for a name, and for a praise, and for a glory (Jer. 13:11), that being called out of darkness into his marvelous light, to be to him a peculiar people, we may show forth the praises of him that hath called us (1 Pet. 2:9).

O that we may be thy children, the work of thy hands, that we may sanctify thy name, and sanctify the Holy One of Jacob, and fear the God of Israel (Isa. 29:23), and may be to the praise of his glory (Eph. 1:12).

Enable us as we have received the gift, so to minister the same, as good stewards of the manifold grace of God, that God in all things may be glorified through Jesus Christ: And if we suffer, enable us to suffer as Christians, and to glorify God therein (1 Pet. 4:10-11,16); for this is our earnest expectation and hope, that always Jesus Christ may be magnified in our bodies, in life and death (Phil. 1:20).

Lord, enable others to glorify thee, even the strong people to glorify thee, and the city of the terrible nations to fear thee (Isa. 25:3); but especially let the Lord be magnified from the border of Israel (Mal. 1:5). Let them glorify the Lord in the east, even the Lord God of Israel in the isles of the sea (Isa. 24:15). O let all nations, whom thou hast made, come and worship before thee, O Lord, and glorify thy name: for thou art great and dost wondrous things, thou art God alone (Ps. 86:9-10).

O let the Gentiles glorify God for his mercy, let his name be known among the Gentiles, and let them rejoice with his people (Rom. 15:9-10), O let thy name be great among the Gentiles (Mal. 1:11), and let all the ends of the world remember and turn to the Lord, and all kindreds of the nations worship before thee; and let them declare thy righteousness to a people that shall be born (Ps. 22:27, 31).

Lord, do thou thyself dispose of all things to thy own glory, both as King of nations, and King of saints (Jer. 10:7; Rev. 15:3): Do all according to the counsel of thy own will (Eph. 1:11), that thou mayest magnify thyself, and sanctify thyself, and mayest be known in the eyes of many nations, that thou art the Lord (Ezek. 38:23). O sanctify thy great name, which has been profaned among the heathen, and let them know that thou art the Lord, when thou shalt be sanctified in them (Ezek. 36:23).

Father, glorify thine own name: Thou hast glorified it, glorify it yet again (John 12:28): Father, glorify thy Son, that thy Son also may glorify thee (John 17:1). O Give him a name above every name (Phil. 2:9), and in all places, in all things let him have the pre-eminence (Col. 1:18).

Lord, what wilt thou do for thy great name (Josh. 7:9)? Do this for thy great name: Pour out of thy Spirit upon all flesh (Joel 2:28); and let the word of Christ dwell richly in the hearts of all (Col. 3:16). Be thou exalted, O Lord, among the heathen, be thou exalted in the earth (Ps. 46:10). Be thou exalted, O God, above the heavens, let thy glory be above all the earth (Ps.

57:11). Be thou exalted, O Lord, in thine own strength, so will we sing and praise thy power (Ps. 21:13). Do great things with thy glorious and everlasting arm, to make unto thyself a glorious and everlasting name (Isa. 63:12,14).

O let thy name be magnified for ever, saying, The Lord of hosts is the God of Israel, even a God to Israel (1 Chron. 17:24).

3. Thy kingdom come.

In order to the sanctifying and glorifying of thy holy name, Father in heaven, let thy kingdom come, for thine is the kingdom, O Lord, and thou art exalted as head above all: Both riches and honour come of thee; thou reignest over all, and in thine hand is power and might, and in thine hand it is to make great, and to give strength unto all (1 Chron. 29:11-12). And we desire to speak of the glorious majesty of thy kingdom, for it is an everlasting kingdom, and thy dominion endures throughout all generations (Ps. 145:11, 13).

Thou rulest by thy power for ever, thine eyes behold the nations. O let not the rebellious exalt themselves (Ps. 66:7), but through the greatness of thy power let thine enemies submit themselves unto thee (Ps. 66:3).

O make it to appear that the kingdom is thine, and that thou art the governor among the nations (Ps. 22:28), so evident, that they may say among the heathen, The Lord reigneth (Ps. 96:10); that all men may fear, and may declare the works of God (Ps. 64:9), and may say, Verily, he is a God that judgeth in the earth (Ps. 58:11). Make all the kings of the earth to know the heavens do rule, even that the Most High ruleth in the kingdom of men, and giveth it to whomsoever he will, and to praise, and to extol, and honour the King of heaven, all those works are truth, and his ways judgment, and those that walk in pride he is able to abase (Dan. 4:25-26, 37).

O let the kingdom of thy grace come more and more in the world, that kingdom of God which cometh not with observation, that kingdom of God, which is within men (Luke 17:20-21). Let it be like leaven in the world, diffusing its relish, till the whole be leavened, and like a grain of mustard-seed, which, though it be the least of all seeds, yet, when it is grown, is the greatest among herbs (Matt. 13:31-33).

Let the kingdoms of the world become the kingdoms of the Lord, and of his Christ: Take unto thyself thy great power, and reign, though the nations be angry (Rev. 11:15, 17). Set up thy throne there where Satan's seat is (Rev 2:13), let every thought be brought into obedience to thee (2 Cor. 10:5), and let the law of thy kingdom be magnified and honourable. (Isa. 42:21).

Let that kingdom of God, which is not in word but in power, be set up in all the churches of Christ (1 Cor. 4:20): Send forth the rod of thy strength out of thy Zion, and rule by the beauty of holiness (Ps 110:2-3).

Where the strong man armed hath long kept his palace, and his goods are in peace, let Christ, who is stronger than he, come upon him, and take from him all his armour, wherein he trusted, and divide the spoil (Luke 11:21-22).

O give to the Son of man dominion and glory, and a kingdom, that all people, nations and languages may serve him, and the judgment may be given to the saints of the Most High (Dan. 7:14, 22).

Let the kingdom of thy grace come more and more in our land, and the places where we live. There let the word of God have free course, and be glorified (2 Thess. 3:1), and let not the kingdom of God be taken from us, as we have deserved it should, and given to a nation bringing forth the fruits thereof (Matt. 21:43).

Let the kingdom of thy grace come into our hearts, that they may be the temples of the Holy Ghost (1 Cor. 3:16). Let no iniquity have dominion over us (Ps. 119:133). Overturn, overturn, overturn the power of corruption there, and let him come whose right our hearts are, and give them to him (Ezek 21:27); make us willing, more and more willing in the day of thy power (Ps. 110:3). Rule in us by the power of truth, that being of the truth, we may always hear Christ's voice (John 18:37), and may not only call him Lord, Lord, but do the things that he saith (Luke 6:46). And let the love of Christ command us, and constrain us (2 Cor. 5:14), and his fear be before our eyes, that we sin not (Exod. 20:20).

O let the kingdom of thy glory be hastened; we believe it will come; we look for the Saviour, the Lord Jesus (Phil. 3:20), to come in the clouds of heaven with power and great glory (Matt. 24:30); we hope that he shall appear to our joy (Isa. 66:5), we love his appearing (2 Tim. 4:8); we are looking for, and hasting to the coming of the day of God (2 Pet. 3:12); make us ready for it (Matt. 24:44), that we may then lift up our heads with joy, knowing that our redemption draws nigh (Luke 21:28). And, O that we may have such first-fruits of the Spirit, as that we ourselves may groan within ourselves, waiting for the adoption, even the redemption of our body (Rom. 8:23); and may have a desire to depart, and to be with Christ, which is best of all (Phil. 1:23).

Blessed Jesus, be with thy ministers and people (as

thou hast said) always even unto the end of the world
(Matt. 28:20): And then (as thou hast said) surely I come
quickly; even so come, Lord Jesus, come quickly (Rev.
22:20): When the mystery of God shall be finished (Rev
10:7), make haste our beloved, and be thou like to a
roe, or to a young hart, upon the mountains of spices
(Cant. 8:14).

4. *Thy Will be done on Earth, as it is in Heaven.*

And as an evidence that thy kingdom comes, and in
order to the sanctifying of thy name, Father in heaven,
let thy holy will be done. We know, O Lord, that
whatsoever thou pleaseth, that thou dost in heaven and
in earth, in the sea, in all deep places (Ps. 135:6): thy
counsel shall stand, and thou wilt do all thy pleasure
(Isa. 46:10); even so be it, holy Father, not our will,
but thine be done (Luke 22:42). As thou hast thought,
so let it come to pass, and as thou hast purposed, let it
stand (Isa. 46:11). Do all according to the counsel of
thine one will (Eph. 1:11). Make even those to serve
thy purposes that have not known thee, and that mean
not so, neither doth their heart think so (Isa. 10:7).

Father, let thy will be done concerning us, and ours
(Isa. 10:7): Behold, here we are: it is the Lord, let him
do to us as seemeth good to him (2 Sam. 15:26): The
will of the Lord be done (Acts 21:14). O give us to
submit to thy will in conformity to the example of the
Lord Jesus, who said, Not as I will, but as thou wilt
(Matt. 26:39), and to say, The Lord gave and the Lord
hath taken away. Blessed be the name of the Lord (Job
1:21). Shall we receive good at the hand of the Lord,
and shall we not receive evil also? (Job 2:10).

Father, let the scriptures be fulfilled (Matt. 26:56);
the scriptures of the prophets, which cannot be broken

(John 10:35). Though heaven and earth pass away, let not one jot or tittle of thy word pass away (Matt. 5:18). Do what is written in the scriptures of truth (Dan. 10:21); and let it appear that for ever, O Lord, thy word is settled in heaven (Ps. 119:89).

Father, give grace to each of us to know and do the will of our Father which is in heaven (Matt. 12:50). This is the will of God, even our sanctification (1 Thess. 4:3). Now the God of peace sanctify us wholly (1 Thess. 5:23). O let us be filled with the knowledge of thy will in all wisdom and spiritual understanding (Col. 1:9), and make us perfect in every good work to do thy will (Heb. 13:21). O let the time past of our life suffice us to have wrought the will of the flesh (1 Pet. 4:3), and to have walked according to the course of this world (Eph. 2:2). And from henceforth grant that it may always be our meat and drink to do the will of our Father, and to finish his work (John 4:34); not to do our own will, but his that sent us (John 6:38), that we may be of those that shall enter into the kingdom (Matt. 7:21) of heaven and not those that shall be beaten with many stripes (Luke 12:47).

Lord, give grace to others also to know and do thy will; to prove what is the good, and acceptable and perfect will of God (Rom. 12:2), not to be unwise, but understanding what the will of the Lord is (Eph. 5:17); and then give them to stand perfect and complete in all the will of God (Col. 4:12): And let us all serve our generations according to that will (Acts 13:36).

And when we have done the will of God, let us inherit the promises (Heb. 10:36); and let that part of the will of God be done; Lord, let the word which thou hast spoken concerning thy servants be established for ever, and do as thou hast said (1 Chron. 17:23).

We rejoice that thy will is done in heaven: that the holy angels do thy commandments, and always hearken to the voice of thy word (Ps. 103:20); that they always behold the face of our Father (Matt. 18:10). And we lament it, that thy will is so little done on earth, so many of the children of men being led captive by Satan at his will (2 Tim. 2:26). O that this earth may be made more like to heaven! and saints more like to the holy angels! and that we who hope to be shortly as the angels of God in heaven (Matt. 22:30), may now, like them, not rest from praising him (Rev. 4:8): may now, like them, resist and withstand Satan (Dan. 10:13); may be as a flame of fire (Ps. 104:4), and fly swiftly, and may go straight forward whithersoever the Spirit goes (Dan. 9:21; Ezek. 1:9,12), may minister for the good of others (Heb. 1:14), and thus may come into communion with the innumerable company of angels (Heb. 12:22).

5. Give us this day our daily bread.

Thou O God, who hath appointed us to seek first the kingdom of God and the righteousness thereof, hast promised that if we do so, other things shall be added unto us (Matt. 6:33): and therefore having prayed for the sanctifying of thy name, the coming of thy kingdom, and the doing of thy will, we next pray, Father in heaven, give us this day, and day by day our daily bread (Luke 11:3).

Remove far from us vanity and lies; give us neither poverty nor riches; feed us with food convenient for us, lest we be full and deny thee, and say, Who is the Lord? or lest we be poor and steal, and take the name of our God in vain (Prov. 30:8-9).

Lord, we ask not for dainties, for they are deceitful meat (Prov. 23:3); nor do we pray that we may fare sumptuously every day, for we would not in our lifetime receive our good things (Prov. 20:17); but we pray for that bread which is necessary to strengthen man's heart (Ps. 104:15). We desire not to eat the bread of deceit (Prov. 20:17), nor to drink any stolen waters (Prov. 9:17), nor would we eat the bread of idleness (Prov. 31:27), but that if it be thy will we may eat the labour of our own hands (Ps. 128:2), that with quietness we may work, and eat our own bread (2 Thess. 3:12); and having food and raiment, give us to be therewith content (1 Tim. 6:8), and to say, we have all, and abound (Phil. 4:18).

Bless, Lord, our substance, and accept the work of our hands (Deut. 33:11); and give us the wherewithal to provide for our own, even for those of our own house (1 Tim. 5:8), and to leave an inheritance, as far as is just, to our children's children (Prov. 13:22). Let the beauty of the Lord our God be upon us, prosper thou the work of our hands upon us, yea, the work of our hands establish thou it (Ps. 90:17). Bless, Lord, our land with the precious things of the earth, and the fulness thereof; but above all let us have the good-will of him that dwelt in the bush, even the blessing that was upon the head of Joseph, and upon the crown of the head of him that was separated from his brethren (Deut. 33:13, 16).

But if the fig-tree should not blossom, and there should be no fruit in the vine; if the labour of the olive should fail, and the fields should yield no meat; if the flock should be cut off from the fold, and there should be no herd in the stall, yet let us have grace to rejoice in the Lord, and to joy in the God of our salvation (Hab. 3:17-18).

Father, we ask not for bread for a great while to

come, but that we may have this day our daily bread; for we would learn, and the Lord teach us not to take thought for the morrow, what we shall eat, or what we shall drink, or wherewithal we shall be clothed, but we cast the care upon thee, our heavenly Father, who knowest that we have need of all these things; who feedest the fowls of the air, though they sow not, neither do they reap, and wilt much more feed us (Matt. 6:31-32), who are of more value than many sparrows (Matt. 10:31).

Nor do we pray for daily bread for ourselves only but for others also. O satisfy thy poor with bread (Ps. 132:15); Let all that walk righteously and speak uprightly dwell on high: Let the place of their defence be the munition of rocks, let bread be given to them, and let their waters be sure (Isa. 33:15-16).

6. And forgive us our debts as we forgive our debtors.
And, Lord, as duly as we pray every day for our daily bread, we pray for the forgiveness of our sins: For we are all guilty before God, have all sinned, and have come short of the glory of God (Rom. 3:19, 23). In many things we all offend every day (Jas. 3:2): Who can tell how oft he offends? If thou shouldest mark iniquities, O Lord, who shall stand? But there is forgiveness with thee, that thou mayest be feared (Ps. 130:3-4). God be merciful to us sinners (Ps. 51:1).

We have wasted our Lord's goods (Luke 16:1), we have buried the talents we were entrusted with (Matt. 25:18), nor have we rendered again according to the benefit done unto us, and thus we came to be in debt (2 Chron. 32:25). The Scripture has concluded us all under sin (Gal. 3:22); we have done such things as are worthy of death (Rom. 1:32); things for which the wrath of

God comes upon the children of disobedience (Eph. 5:6). Our debt is more than ten thousand talents. It is a great debt; and we have nothing to pay, so far are we from being able to say, Have patience with us, and we will pay thee all (Matt. 18:24-26, 32). Justly therefore might our adversary deliver us to the judge, and the judge to the officer, to be cast into prison, the prison of hell, till we should pay the last farthing (Matt. 5:25, 29).

But blessed be God, there is a way found out of agreeing with our adversary; for if any man sin, we have an advocate with the Father, even Jesus Christ the righteous, and he is the propitiation for our sins (1 John 2:1-2).

For his sake, we pray thee, blot out all our transgressions (Ps. 51:1), and enter not into judgment with us (Ps. 143:2). He is our surety (Heb. 7:22), who restored that which he took not away (Ps. 69:4), that blessed days-man, who hath laid his hand upon us both (Job 9:33), through him let us be reconciled unto God (2 Cor. 5:20), and let the hand-writing which was against, which was contrary to us, be blotted out, and taken out of the way, being nailed to the cross of Christ, that we may be quickened together with Christ, having all our trespasses forgiven us (Col. 2:13-14). Be thou merciful to our unrighteousness, and our sins and our iniquities do thou remember no more (Heb. 8:12).

And give us, we pray thee, to receive the atonement (Rom. 5:11), to know that our sins are forgiven us (1 John 2:12): Speak peace to us (Ps. 85:8), and make us to hear joy and gladness (Ps. 51:8). Let the blood of Christ thy son cleanse us from all sin (1 John 1:7), and purge our consciences from dead works, to serve the living God (Heb. 9:14).

And as an evidence that thou hast forgiven our sins, we pray thee, give us grace to forgive our enemies, to love them that hate us, and bless them that curse us (Matt. 5:44); for we acknowledge, that if we forgive not men their trespasses, neither will our Father forgive our trespasses (Matt. 6:15): And therefore we forgive, Lord, we desire heartily to forgive (Mark 11:25), if we have a quarrel against any, even as Christ forgave us (Col. 3:13). Far be it from us to say, that we will recompense evil (Prov. 20:22), or that we should avenge ourselves (Rom. 12:19). But we pray that all bitterness, and wrath, and anger, and clamour, and evil speaking may be put away from us, with all malice; and that we may be kind one to another, and tender-hearted, forgiving one another, even as God for Christ's sake, we hope, hath forgiven us (Eph. 4:31-32). O make us merciful, as our Father who is in heaven is merciful (Matt. 5:7), who hath promised that with the merciful he will shew himself merciful (Ps. 18:25).

7. And lead us not into temptation, but deliver us from evil.

And Lord, forasmuch as there is in us a bent to backslide from thee (Hos. 11:7), so that when our sins are forgiven, we are ready to return again to folly (Ps. 85:8), we pray that thou wilt not only forgive us our debts, but take care of us, that we may not offend any more (Job 34:31). Lord, lead us not into temptation. We know that no man can say when he is tempted, that he is tempted of God, for God tempteth not any man (Jas. 1:13); but we know that God is able to make all grace abound towards us (2 Cor. 9:8), and to keep us from falling, and present us faultless (Jude 24). We therefore pray that thou wilt never give us up to our own heart's lust, to walk in our own counsels (Ps. 81:12), but restrain Satan, that roaring lion that goes about seeking whom he may devour (1 Pet. 5:8); and grant that we may not be ignorant of his devices (2 Cor. 2:11). O let not Satan have us to sift us as wheat; or however, let not our faith fail (Luke 22:31-32). Let not the messengers of Satan be permitted to buffet us; but if they be, let thy grace be sufficient for us that where we are weak, there we may be strong (2 Cor. 12:7, 9-10), and may be more than conquerors through him that loved us (Rom. 8:37). And, the God of peace tread Satan under our feet, and do it shortly (Rom. 16:20). And since we wrestle not against flesh and blood, but against principalities and powers, and the rulers of the darkness of this world, let us be strong in the Lord, and in the power of his might (Eph. 6:10, 12).

Lord, grant that we may never enter into temptation (Matt. 26:41), but having prayed may set a watch (Neh. 4:9), and let thy wise and good providence so order all our affairs and all events that are concerning us, that no temptation may take us but such as is common to men, and that we may never be tempted above what we are able to discern, resist, and overcome through the grace of God (1 Cor. 10:13). Lord, do not lay any stumbling block before us, that we should fall upon them and perish (Jer. 6:21). Let nothing be an occasion of falling to us (Rom. 14:14), but give us that great peace which they have that love thy law, whom nothing shall offend (Ps. 119:165).

And lead us, we pray thee, into all truth (John 16:13); lead us in thy truth, and teach us, for thou art the God of our salvation (Ps. 24:4-5). Show us thy ways, O God, and teach us thy paths, the paths of righteousness: O lead us in those paths for thy name's sake, that so we may be led beside the still waters (Ps. 23:2-3).

And deliver us, we pray thee, from the evil one; keep us that the wicked one touch us not (1 John 5:18), that he sow not his tares in the field of our hearts (Matt. 13:25), that we be not ensnared by his wiles, or wounded by his fiery darts (Eph. 6:11, 16), let the word of God abide in us, that we may be strong, and may overcome the wicked one (1 John 2:14).

Deliver us from every evil thing, we pray, that we may do no evil (2 Cor. 13:7): O deliver us from every evil work (2 Tim. 4:18), save us from our sins (Matt. 1:21), redeem us from all iniquity (Titus 2:14), especially the sin that doth most easily beset us (Heb. 12:1).

Hide pride from us (Job 33:17); remove from us the way of lying (Ps. 119:29); let us not eat of sinners' dainties (Ps. 114:4): incline our hearts to thy testimonies, and not to covetousness (Ps. 119:36); and keep us that we never speak unadvisedly with our lips (Ps. 106:33). But especially keep back thy servant from presumptuous sins, let them not have dominion over us (Ps. 19:13).

Preserve us, we pray thee, that no evil thing may befall us (Ps. 91:10), and keep us from evil, that it may not hurt us (Ps. 121:7). O thou that savest by thy right hand them which put their trust in thee, from those that rise up against them, shew us thy marvelous loving-kindness, and keep us as the apple of thine eye, hide us under the shadow of thy wings (Ps. 17:7-8). Keep that which we commit unto thee (2 Tim. 1:12). Thou that hast delivered, dost deliver (2 Cor. 1:10), and we trust and pray, that thou wilt yet deliver, wilt deliver us from all our fears (Ps. 34:4). O make us to dwell safely, and grant that we may be quiet from the fear of evil (Prov. 1:33). And bring us safe at last to thy holy mountain, where there is no pricking briar, or grieving thorn, nothing to hurt or destroy (Ezek. 28:24; Isa. 11:9).

8. For thine is the Kingdom, the Power, and the Glory, for ever. Amen.

Father, in heaven, let thy kingdom come, for thine is the kingdom, thou art God in heaven, and rulest over all the kingdoms of the heathen (2 Chron. 20:6): Let thy will be done, for thine is the power, and there is nothing too hard for thee (Jer. 32:17): Let thy name be sanctified, for thine is the glory, and thou has set thy glory above the heavens (Ps. 8:1).

Father in heaven, supply our wants, pardon our sins, and preserve us from evil, for thine is the kingdom, the power, and the glory, and thou art Lord over all, who art rich to all that call upon thee (Rom. 10:12); None can forgive sins but thou only (Mark 2:7), let thy power be great in pardoning our sins (Num. 14:17); And since it is the glory of God to pardon sin, and to help the helpless (Prov. 25:2), help us, O God of our salvation: for the glory of thy name deliver us, and purge away our sins, for thy name's sake (Ps. 79:9).

We desire in all our prayers to praise thee, for thou art great and greatly to be praised (Ps. 145:3). We praise thy kingdom, for it is an everlasting kingdom, and endures throughout all generations (Ps. 145:13), and the sceptre of thy kingdom is a right sceptre (Ps. 56:6-7): Thou lovest righteousness, and hatest wickedness: To thee belongeth mercy, and thou renderest to every man according to his works (Ps. 62:12). We praise thy power, for thou hast a mighty arm, strong is thy hand and high is thy right hand, and yet judgment and justice are the habitation of thy throne, mercy and truth shall go before thy face (Ps. 89:13-14). We praise thy glory, for the glory of the Lord shall endure for ever (Ps. 104:31). Glory be to the Father, to the Son, and to the Holy Ghost: As it was in the beginning, is now, and ever shall be. O let God be praised in his sanctuary, and praised in the firmament of his power; let him be praised for his mighty acts, and praised according to his excellent greatness. Let every thing that hath breath praise the Lord (Ps. 150:1-2,6). Hallelujah.

And forasmuch as we know that he heareth us, and whatsoever we ask, according to his will, in faith, we have the petitions that we desired of him (1 John 5:15), we will triumph in his praise (Ps. 106:47). Now know we that the Lord heareth his anointed (Ps. 20:6), and for his sake will hear us from his holy heaven, with the saving strength of his right hand; and therefore in token not only of our desire, but of our assurance to be heard in Christ's name, we say, *Amen, Amen.*

Bibliography

I
Commentaries on Matthew
and/or the Sermon on the Mount:

Barclay, William. *The Gospel of Matthew – Vol. 2 (Chs. 1–10)*. Philadelphia, Pennsylvania: The Westminster Press, 1958

Boice, James M. *The Sermon on the Mount*. Grand Rapids, Michigan: Zondervan Publishing House, 1972

Bonhoeffer, Dietrich. *The Cost of Discipleship*. New York: MacMillan Publishing Company, Inc., 1937, 1959

Calvin, John. *A Harmony of the Gospels, Matthew, Mark, and Luke, vol. 1,* Grand Rapids, Michigan: Eerdmans Publishing Company, 1555, 1972

Carson, D. A. 'Matthew' In *The Expositor's Bible Commentary – Vol. 8*. ed. Frank E.Gæbelein, 1-599. Grand Rapids, Michigan: Zondervan, 1984

Dickson, David. *A Brief Exposition of Jesus Christ According to Matthew*. Edinburgh: The Banner of Truth Trust, 1647, 1981

Ferguson, Sinclair B. *Kingdom Life in a Fallen World*. Colorado Springs, Colorado: Navpress, 1986

France, R. T. *Tyndale New Testament Commentaries –
Matthew.* Grand Rapids, Michigan: Eerdmans
Publishing Co., 1985

Henry, Matthew. *A Commentary on the Whole Bible –
Vol. 5.* Iowa Falls, Iowa: World Bible Publishers,
1721, n.d.

Hill, David. *The Gospel of Matthew.* New Century Bible.
Grand Rapids, Michigan: Eerdmans; London:
Marshall, Morgan and Scott, 1972

Keener, Craig S. *A Commentary on the Gospel of
Matthew.* Grand Rapids, Michigan; Cambridge, UK:
Eerdmans, 1999

Lloyd Jones, D. Martyn. *Studies in the Sermon on the
Mount, Vol. 2.* London, England: Inter-Varsity
Fellowship, 1960

Morris, Leon. *The Gospel According to Matthew.* Grand
Rapids, Michigan: Eerdmans Publishing Co., 1992

Plummer, Alfred. *An Exegetical Commentary on the
Gospel According to St. Matthew.* Grand Rapids,
Michigan: Eerdmans Publishing Company, 1909,
1953

Ryle, J. C. *Expository Thoughts on the Gospels – Matthew.*
Cambridge, England: James Clarke & Co. Ltd.,
1856, 1974

Stott, John R. W. *The Message of the Sermon on the
Mount.* Downers Grove, Illinois: Inter-Varsity Press,
1978

Tasker, R. V. G. *Tyndale New Testament Commentaries
– The Gospel According to St. Matthew.* Grand Rapids,
Michigan: Eerdmans Publishing Company, 1961

II
Books on the Lord's Prayer:

Blaiklock, E. M. *The Positive Power of Prayer*. Glendale, California: G/L Regal Publications, 1974

Pink, A. W. *The Beatitudes and the Lord's Prayer*. Grand Rapids, Michigan: Baker Book House, 1979, 1982

Kelly, Douglas F. *If God Already Knows, Why Pray?* Brentwood, Tennessee: Wolgemuth and Hyatt, 1989

Ryken, Philip G. *The Prayer of Our Lord*. Wheaton, Illinois: Crossway Books, 2002

Thomas, Derek. *Praying the Saviour's Way*. Great Britain: Christian Focus Publications, 2002

Thomson, James G. S. S. *The Praying Christ*. Grand Rapids, Michigan: Eerdmans, 1959

Watson, Thomas. *The Lord's Prayer*. London: The Banner of Truth Trust, 1692, 1965

Witsius, Herman. *The Lord's Prayer*. Phillipsburg, New Jersey: Presbyterian and Reformed Publishing Company, 1680(?), 1994

Wright, N. T. *The Lord and His Prayer*. Grand Rapids, Michigan: Eerdmans, 1996, 1997

III
Books on Prayer:

Bounds, E. M. *Power Through Prayer* (in *The Complete Works of E. M. Bounds on Prayer*). Grand Rapids, Michigan: Baker Book House, 1912, 1990

Bunyan, John. *Prayer*. London: The Banner of Truth Trust, 1662, 1965

Coggan, Donald. *The Prayers of the New Testament.* New York: Harper and Row Publishers, 1967

Hallesby, O. *Prayer.* London:Inter-Varsity Fellowship, 1948, 1955

Henry, Matthew. *A Method for Prayer,* ed. J. Ligon Duncan III. Greenville, South Carolina: Reformed Academic Press, 1712, 1994

Johnson, Terry ed. *Leading in Worship.* Oak Ridge, Tennessee: The Covenant Foundation, 1996

Murray, Andrew. *With Christ in the School of Prayer.* New Kensington, Pensylvania: Whitaker House, 1885, 1981

Old, Hughes Oliphant. *Leading in Prayer.* Grand Rapids, Michigan: Eerdmans, 1995

Packer, J. I. *I Want to be a Christian.* Eastbourne, Sussex: Tyndale House, 1977

Pratt, Richard L. Jr. *Pray With Your Eyes Open.* Phillipsburg, New Jersey: Presbyterian and Reformed Publishing, 1987

Ryle, J. C. *A Call to Prayer.* Grand Rapids, Michigan: Baker Book House, 1878, 1976

Unknown, *The Kneeling Christian.* Grand Rapids, Michigan: Zondervan, 1971

Watts, Isaac. *A Guide to Prayer.* Edinburgh: The Banner of Truth Trust, 1715, 2001

Persons Index

Subject Index

Scripture Index

WHEN GRACE COMES ALIVE

1 John (*cont*)
5:14-15	44, 215
5:15	248
5:18	246

3 John
| 2 | 130 |
| 9 | 175 |

Jude
| 24 | 67, 172, 244 |

Revelation
1:17	35
2:13	236
4:8	240
4:9-11	104
4:10	35

5:8	35
5:14	35, 104
6:10	112
10:7	238
11:15	114, 236
11:16	35
11:17	236
15:3	234
21:1-6	126
22:20	238

When Grace comes Home

How the doctrines of grace change your life
Terry Johnson

How does 'Grace' become a part of your life so that God becomes real to you in every situation?

Terry Johnson has provided a splendid work on how right theology bears upon our worship, character, suffering, witness and growth in the Christian life. 'whether evangelicals know it or not, their future as a viable movement depends upon the rediscovery of such God-honoring theology.

**The late Dr James M Boice,
Tenth Presbyterian, Philadelphia**

Rarely can the vitamin content of sweet, strong, classic pastoral Calvinism have been made so plain and palatable as it is here.

**J I Packer,
Regent's College, Vancouver**

Terry Johnson... enriches our understanding of the difference that the doctrines of Grace not only make to the way we do theology, but also for the ways in which we serve God and love our neighbors.

**D G Hart,
Associate Professor of Church History,
Westminster Theological Seminary**

The fine book proves for Christians something that they should already know, but often miss: theology matters! With much practical wisdom and help for Christian thinking and living, this book makes good application of good theology.

**Rev Dr Robert Godfrey,
Westminster West Theological Seminary**

ISBN 1 85792 5394

When Grace Transforms
The character of Christ's disciples envisioned in the beatitudes
Terry Johnson

The Beatitudes have found, in Terry Johnson, the expositor we have all been waiting for, and they become, in his hands, a statement of Christian ethics as profound as it is readable. He is as faithful in bruising as in uplifting, but, being a true pastor, even his bruises have a velvet and healing touch.

Alec Motyer

My 'Sermon on the Mount' note book is now crammed with Johnsonisms—*pithy one-liners that get to the heart of what Jesus meant by adorning the righteousness of the kingdom of God. This is where preaching and teaching needs to go.*

Derek W H Thomas
Reformed Theological Seminary, Jackson, Mississippi

...a clarion call to discipleship in depth.

J I Packer
Regent College, Vancouver

...What a timely emphasis for a generation long on license and short on character.

J Ligon Duncan III
First Presbyterian Church, Jackson, Mississippi

...a challenge to Christian counter-culture on both sides of the Atlantic.
Philip H Hacking

Terry explains each of the beatitudes, showing both *what they don't mean, and what they do*. His conclusions are strong, challenging, and immensely practical.

Let Jesus change your attitudes

ISBN 1 85792 7702

The Family Worship Book
A Resource book for Family Devotions
Terry Johnson

Do you struggle to provide enjoyable, meaningful and spiritual times of family devotions? Do you avoid the whole subject but have the nagging thought that you should be doing something? Here is the solution, a book that will give you the impetus to start.

Terry Johnson (who gave us Leading in Worship) has now provided us with a superb resource for family religion: The Family Worship Book. Johnson provides a brief but compelling argument for the importance of family worship, but then takes those he has convinced in theory to the next step: actually putting it into practice!

In a day and age when family worship is a rarity, and in which parents who are called to lead in it are not likely to have had personal experience of it in their own upbringing, Johnson's book will prove to be an invaluable aid. I have known many parents who feel the responsibility to lead the family in devotional exercises and who genuinely desire to be faithful in that covenantal responsibility, but who do not seem to know what to do or how to begin.

Here's the antidote. I hope that this book will be widely circulated and used among God's people. We may not expect a climate of serious spirituality to return to our churches until family religion again becomes a norm. May the Lord use this book to bring about a revival of family worship in our land.

J Ligon Duncan, III
First Presbyterian Church, Jackson, Mississippi

ISBN 1 85792 4010